Microsoft Visio

Step by Step Ultimate Guide for Beginners and Expert

SMITH ROSS

Table of Contents

xi

Chapter 1

Creation of Visio Diagram

Hit the Ground Running with Visio

Have you ever encountered files and folders filled with complex text and tables that are difficult to decipher? Visio offers a solution to this problem. With Visio, you can transform intricate text and tables into visually engaging diagrams that effectively convey information. Whether it's organizational charts, network diagrams, workflows, or architectural designs, Visio provides various diagram types to suit your needs. To begin using Visio effectively, it's essential to grasp three fundamental concepts: utilizing templates, arranging and linking objects, and modifying shapes.

Before delving into these processes, let's cover some essential concepts that beginners need to grasp.

Determine the Different Editions of Visio

The initial release of Visio dates back to 1992 under the Shakespeare company, later renamed Visio Corporation. In 2000, Microsoft acquired Visio, leading to the introduction of numerous Visio versions over the years. Presently, all commercial SKUs of Microsoft 365 include a streamlined version of Visio known as Visio in Microsoft 365. Additionally, there are two subscription-based SKUs available: Visio Plan 2 grants access to both the web app and desktop program, while Visio Plan 1 provides access solely to the Visio web app.

Starting from Visio 2013 for Windows, Microsoft has provided Visio in both professional and standard editions. The Professional edition offers an extensive range of templates suited for complex diagrams, layouts, and features facilitating the linking of diagrams to data sources for graphical representation. Despite sharing the same interface, the Standard and Professional editions differ in capabilities. The Professional edition encompasses additional features such as subprocesses, intelligent rules, and three distinct diagram types. Furthermore, Visio Professional is also available as part of an Office365 subscription, thus representing a third edition option.

Explore the Latest Functionalities in Visio

The latest iteration of Visio, Visio 2021, boasts a vibrant and modern interface, improved connectivity, enhanced collaboration features, and heightened document security measures.

Below are some of the Latest Features in Visio Diagrams:

- **Modern Templates:** Visio now offers contemporary templates to streamline diagram creation and provide a fresh starting point for projects.

- **Improved Connectivity:** Visio 2021 boasts enhanced connectivity options, allowing seamless integration with Microsoft Office apps and external data sources.

- **Real-time Collaboration:** Users can collaborate on Visio diagrams in real-time, enabling multiple team members to work simultaneously and boost productivity.

- **Cloud Storage Integration:** Visio integrates seamlessly with cloud storage services, facilitating easy access and sharing of diagrams from any location.

- **Enhanced Security:** Visio 2021 includes upgraded security features to safeguard diagram data and ensure compliance with privacy regulations.

- **Dynamic gridlines**: Visio's latest feature simplifies the process of arranging shapes on your page. With dynamic gridlines activated, gridlines appear automatically whenever a shape is moved or resized on your canvas. To enable dynamic gridlines, navigate to "**View**" > "**Dynamic Gridlines**" in the ribbon interface.

- **Lasso select tool**: The "**Lasso select**" tool in Visio simplifies the process of selecting multiple shapes on your canvas. By dragging a lasso with your mouse pointer around the desired shapes, you can easily select them. To use this tool, click on the "**Lasso select**" tool in the toolbar located on the left side of the Visio window, or simply press **Shift+F2** on your keyboard. Once activated, you can select shapes by clicking and dragging your mouse cursor over them.

- **Align and distribute option**: In Visio 2021, the align and distribute options have been enhanced for easier access. You can now find them within the contextual tab labeled "**Shape Format**" on the ribbon interface. Simply navigate to "**Shape Format**" > "**Arrange**" > "**Align or Distribute**" to access these options.

- **Publish**: To upload your diagrams to SharePoint for others to access and edit, you can utilize the "Publish to SharePoint" option. Simply follow these steps:

  - Click on "**File**" > "**Share**" > "**Publish Diagram**".

- o You'll be prompted to provide a name, description, and specify a SharePoint location for your diagram.
- **New Azure Stencils and shapes:** There are now additional stencils available to assist you in creating Azure diagrams.

New AWS Stencils and Shapes

Wireframe Diagram for Mobile Apps

A wireframe is a detailed visual depiction of an interface, serving as a blueprint for functionality and content. With Visio wireframe, you can now actualize ideas. These new mobile app templates are ideal for conveying concepts, achieving team consensus, and establishing the foundation for a high-fidelity wireframe.

The latest version of Microsoft Visio Professional 2021 offers a visually refreshing experience with a modern touch. With updated features, it's now easier than ever to create diagrams with a polished and contemporary appearance. Microsoft Visio Professional 2021 remains a powerful yet user-friendly diagramming tool that is definitely worth considering.

Let's Get Started with Visio

When you launch Visio, the start screen greets you with options such as recently opened diagrams and the main start screen.

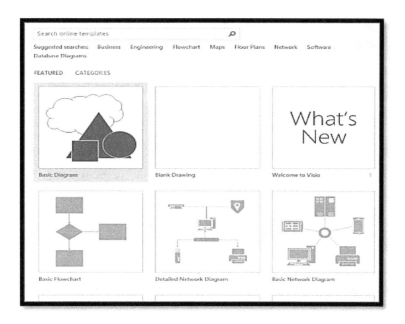

From the Visio start screen, you can create a new diagram. Alternatively, if Visio is already open, you can create a new diagram from the New Page option.

It's important to note that the start screen initially showcases featured templates, which might divert your attention from the categories button.

Before proceeding, it's essential to grasp some standard terms commonly used in Visio.

Sidebar: Familiarize Yourself with the Concepts of shapes,

Masters, Stencils and Templates.

Shape: Item in a Visio drawing page

Basic shapes such as lines, polygons, or images constitute the foundation of shapes. These intelligent objects can modify their appearance or behavior based on alterations in data values, positioning on the page, or the properties of other shapes.

Besides transferring a "Master" from a stencil to the drawing page, there are various methods to construct shapes.

Master: This refers to an object contained within the Visio stencil.

The majority of Visio users rely on the pre-existing masters included in the program or obtain masters from external sources. Additionally, users have the capability to create their own masters.

Stencil: This refers to a combination of masters. In both metric and American unit versions, Visio offers nearly 200 stencils, each containing multiple related masters—sometimes a dozen or more. Stencil examples include furniture, transportation, workflow, network locations and timeline shapes.

Template: A Visio document comprises one or more drawing pages, each with predefined measurements and proportions.

A template typically contains one or more stencils and may incorporate text, shapes, or background pages. It may also include specialized software that functions exclusively within the template.

Workspace: This is where all the Visio windows and settings are consolidated.

The workspace typically includes the drawing window and zoom options for the drawing pages as a basic setup. It often features a Shapes window housing one or more stencils. Additionally, workspace and template-specific windows may include Shape Info, Size & Location, and Pan & Zoom options.

If you leave the default setting unchanged, Visio will save the current on-screen workspace layout along with the documents. Consequently, when you reopen the document later, Visio will restore the workspace to its previous state.

However, despite the distinction between "**shapes**" and "**masters**," individuals often use the term "shapes" to refer to objects within stencils. Interestingly, the windows displaying the stencils can also be termed the "**Shapes window**." However, for clarity within this book, we will predominantly refer to objects within stencils and on the drawing page as shapes.

To initiate a diagram using an existing template, you can opt for one of the following methods.

Note: Searching with a keyword may not yield identical results to selecting a template category that includes the term. For example, opting for the "**Flowchart**" search term may bring up some of the templates available in the dedicated Flowchart template category. **However, it also presents a list of numerous templates, ranging from Visio-specific templates to those tailored for other Office suite programs.**

- Select one of the templates featured in this section. The templates you frequently use are prioritized here, and the thumbnails in this section are displayed dynamically.
- To locate grouped templates, utilize the Category view, which presents templates under distinct categories. In Visio Standard, you'll find categories like Business, Flowchart, General, Maps and Floor Plans, Network, and Scheduling. Visio Professional introduces two additional categories: Engineering and Software, and Database. At the end of the template category list, you'll also find a new entry labeled "New from Existing."

You can select any thumbnail of a Visio diagram currently in use. Visio will then create a copy of the diagram and close the original document. When you choose any template category, you'll see thumbnails for the templates. Here are some of the templates available:

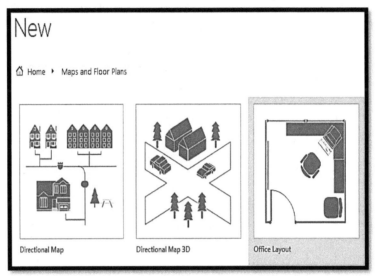

To access more details about the template, you must select the diagram thumbnail. However, to initiate a new diagram, simply double-click the thumbnail.

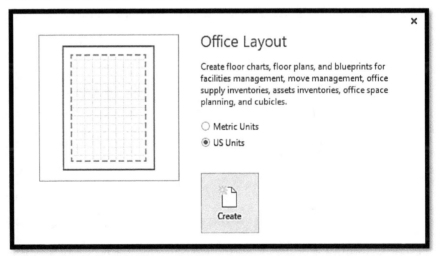

Visio Templates are Available in Two sets of Measurement units

- All measurements are expressed in millimeters or another metric unit. Metric templates adhere to standard paper sizes established by the International Organization for Standardization (ISO), with the typical size being A4. Additionally, other ISO paper and drawing sizes are available in metric templates.
- The standard units of measurement are inches and feet. Diagrams created with US Units use the US 8.5 by 11-inch letter-sized paper, which is common in the United States, as well as some regions of Canada and Mexico. Templates designed for US Units also include typical drawing and paper sizes used in those nations and areas.

The choice offered to you depends on the configuration of your system.

To open a previously used diagram, follow these steps:

- Select the desired diagram from the "**Recent**" column on the Start screen of the Backstage view by clicking its name.

To open a diagram that isn't listed under "**Recent**," you can:

- Select "**Open Other Diagrams**" from the "**Recent**" column.
- Click the location, then select the desired diagram from the "**Open**" page of the Backstage view.

Utilizing a Featured Template

- If the Featured tab is not already open on the Start screen, click the Featured button located above the thumbnails.
- Select one of the following options:

- o Double-click on the thumbnail of a template.
- o Next, click on the thumbnail of the desired template and then select the "Create" button.

To utilize one of the template categories, simply click on the desired category

- ▪ If the Categories tab is not already visible, click the Categories button above the thumbnails on the Start screen to open it.
- ▪ Select the desired category by clicking on its thumbnail.
- ▪ Select one of the following actions:
  - o Double-click the thumbnail of a template to open it.
  - o Click on the desired template thumbnail, then hit the "**Create**" button to select it.

Looking for a Template

Select one of the following options from the Start screen:

- o Enter your search terms into the "**Search for online templates**" box, then hit **Enter**.
- o Select a keyword from the list of suggested searches.

To create a template from an existing diagram

- o If the Categories tab is not selected on the Start screen, click the Categories button.

Select one of the following options:

- o Double-click the thumbnail labeled "**New from Existing**" to proceed.
- o After selecting the "New from Existing" thumbnail, click the "**Create**" button to proceed.

Navigate through the Backstage View to Access various Functions and Settings

Access the backstage view by clicking on the File tab located on the leftmost section of the Visio window. This area serves as the central hub for file management and configuration of Visio settings.

Without a diagram open, only four of the 11 commands in the Backstage view's left pane—New, Open, Account, and Options—are accessible. However, upon opening a diagram, the remaining seven commands become visible.

If you're in the Backstage view with an open diagram, clicking the left-pointing arrow in the upper-left corner of the Visio window will return you to the diagram. If no diagrams are open, clicking the arrow will take you back to the Start screen.

If you're accustomed to using other Office suite applications, navigating the Backstage view in Visio will feel familiar to you. However, there are specific Visio features within the Backstage view that we'll explore in this topic.

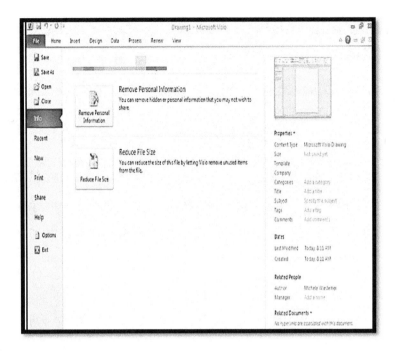

The Info Page

When you open a diagram and click on the File tab, you'll be directed to the Info page.

These are Five keys

- Restrict Permission to this diagram

- Remove personal information

- Reduce file size

- Check compatibility

- Publish options

We will delve into each of these components extensively in the subsequent sections of this book. On the right side of the page, you'll find details about the open document, accompanied by a Properties list where you can examine and adjust document attributes.

Below are Additional Buttons you'll Encounter on the Info Page:

- If the document you open is in read-only mode, you will see the following image on the info page:

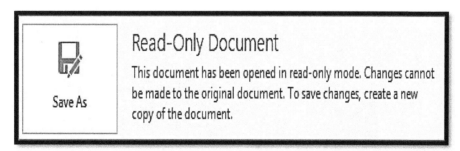

- For earlier versions of Visio, your file will open in compatibility mode, and you will see a "**Convert**" button. If you store a document in SharePoint or a drive, you will see the "**Check Out**" and "**View Version History**" buttons.

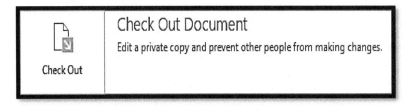

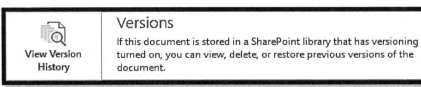

To prevent someone else from making changes to a document you are editing, click the "**Check Out**" button. The "Check Out" button is replaced by a "Check In" button, which you use to indicate that the document is available when you click it. To examine and control a document's most recent and earlier versions, use the "View Version History" button.

The New Page

This resembles both the info page and the start screen. On the start screen, you can view all of the featured templates, as well as the template categories and some online template search options, similar to what you see here.

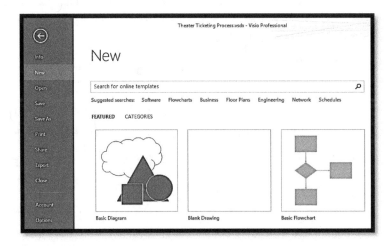

The first thing you'll encounter on the New Page is the featured template.

The Open Page

On the Open Page, you can access various locations to store your diagrams. Once you select a location from the left column, you'll see the diagrams you've recently used or stored there. Additionally, you can add online locations to the list or browse through them to find the specific diagram you want to work with.

The Save Command

When you attempt to exit an unsaved diagram, you'll encounter the Save As page. However, if the diagram has already been saved, selecting "Save" simply updates the changes you've made.

The Save as Page

On this page, you have the option to select a local or online location to save your data. You can also choose from recently accessed folders or click "Browse" to navigate to the desired location for saving your data.

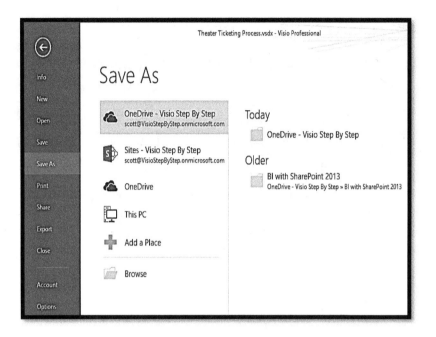

The Print Page

On this page, you'll find the print preview and printing options.

The Share Page

On the Share page, you have two options for sharing your diagram: share with people or share via email.

To email someone a link to your diagram, click "Share with People." For the sharing feature to work, your diagram must be saved in OneDrive or SharePoint. If it isn't, you'll be prompted to save it in one of those places initially.

When your diagram is available online, you can send a link to multiple people using the provided form. Alternatively, you can choose the "Email" button to send diagrams with any options on the right side of the page.

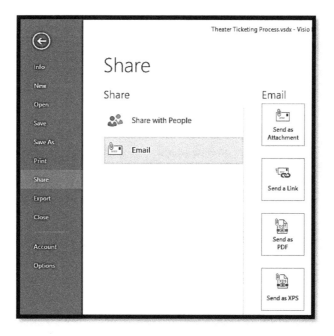

The Export Page

Utilize the export page to create a PDF or XPS document and to save the file in various formats.

The Close Command

When you choose the "**Close**" command, you will close the active diagram, but you will not exit the software entirely.

The Account Page

On the "**Account**" page, you'll find a summary of the information associated with your linked Microsoft account in Visio. To modify the details of your Microsoft account, you can click the link provided within the user information area.

In the "Account" page, you'll find options to modify Visio's and all other Office programs' Office Backgrounds and Themes. Additionally, the "Connected Services" section provides a list of the OneDrive and SharePoint sites you're currently connected to. You can link to more OneDrive and SharePoint sites by clicking the "Add A Service" option. Lastly, clicking the "About Visio" button in the "Product Information" area opens the "About Microsoft Visio" dialog box.

The Visio Options Dialog Box

You can access the Visio Options dialog box, where numerous settings allow you to customize Visio's functionality, by clicking the "**Options**" button. While many Visio users may not need to adjust these settings, exploring the option categories can be beneficial.

The Visio Options dialog box provides a range of operations you can perform to customize your Visio experience. Here are just a few examples of what you can do:

- **General**: By entering your username and initials, you can establish various global parameters, such as Live Preview and color schemes, across all Office applications.
- **Proofing**: This option validates and sets preferences for grammar, spelling and autocorrect.
- **Save**: Specify the default save format for Visio from three options (Visio Document, Visio Macro-Enabled Document, and Visio 2003-2010 Document). Additionally, enable AutoRecover and define the location for your templates.
- **Language**: Adjust the language settings for editing, display, help, and ScreenTip language for images.
- **Advance**: Many options can be configured under the following five headings: Editing, Display, Save/Open, Shape Search, and General.
- **Personalize Ribbon**: This function allows users to create new tabs and commands, as well as add and rearrange commands on existing ribbon tabs.
- **Quick Access Toolbar**: This feature enables users to add or remove the Command button for the Quick Access Toolbar.

- **Trust center**: From this section, users can view and edit macro settings and other trust options.

To access the Backstage view, simply click on the File tab.

Comprehend the Functionality of tool Tabs and Supplementary add-in Tabs

Most tabs in Visio are readily visible, but there are two types of tabs that become visible only when needed.

Utilize Tool Tabs

The tool tab group becomes visible when a particular type of shape is selected on the drawing page, appearing exclusively in that context. Typically positioned to the right of the View tab, these groups do not remain permanently active; thus, clicking the tab may be necessary to reveal its contents. Identified by a colored header, a tool tab group may contain one or more tool tabs beneath it.

As illustrated in the image below, the Picture Tools tab group becomes visible upon inserting or selecting a graphic on a Visio drawing page. Within this group, the Format tool tab, situated on the green Picture Tools page, provides buttons for cropping, rotating, and performing other image-editing operations.

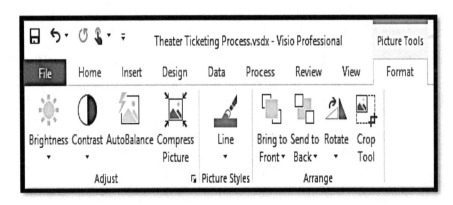

Here's another example: the **Container Tools** tab group, which appears whenever a Visio container is selected or added, is depicted here. On the Format tool tab within the orange Container Tools tab group, you'll find a button for resizing, styling, and managing container membership.

Utilize add-in tabs

Add-in tabs are extensions linked to Visio software, enhancing its functionality. While Microsoft provides certain add-ins with Visio, others are available for purchase from independent software companies.

Tool tabs exhibit distinct appearances and behaviors. The only instance they resemble permanent Visio tabs precisely is when an add-in program is active.

For example, when you create or edit a drawing using one of Visio's organization chart templates, the Org Chart add-in, which is included with Visio, becomes activated. This results in the display of the Org Chart add-in tab.

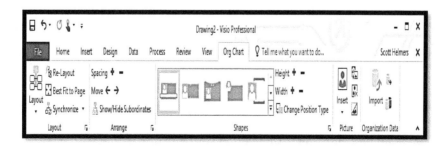

TaskMap represents a third-party add-in, providing straightforward functionalities for process mapping, analysis, and enhancement. Both Visio Standard and Visio Professional are compatible with TaskMap.

Get Started Swiftly by Utilizing Starter Diagrams

Visio templates traditionally offer stencil-filled shapes for creating fresh diagrams. However, even when using a template to initiate a diagram, the new drawing page remains blank, which can make it challenging to determine where to begin.

Visio significantly reduces the workload by providing numerous pre-designed diagrams, complete with appropriately structured and formatted shapes, along with a list of suggestions.

Displayed below is an example of a starting diagram from the Timeline template within the Schedule template group. Clicking on any starter diagram thumbnail allows you to learn more about that specific example diagram and the scenarios in which it could be beneficial.

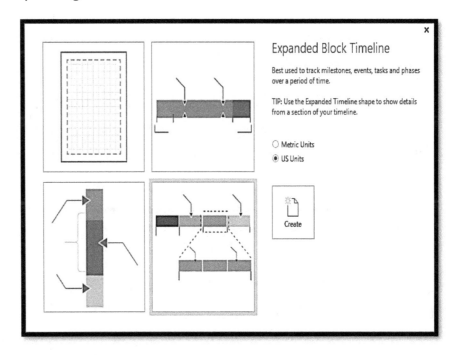

The option for a blank page becomes accessible when you select the thumbnail located in the upper left corner. Upon choosing one of the thumbnails, you'll be presented with a one-page document featuring the starter diagram.

The image below showcases the Expanded Block Timeline diagram.

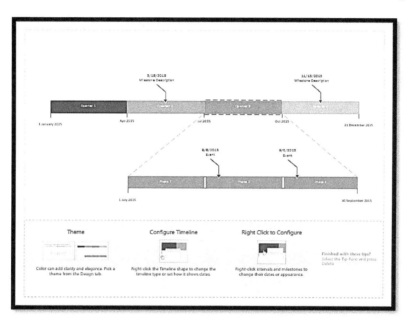

In addition to the diagram itself, the starter diagram contains several other elements. These include the tip pane, which offers general and domain-centered tips. Once you've finished with the tips pane, you can remove it from the page. Additionally, there are starter diagrams accessible within the Visio Starter Diagram.

They are as follows.

- o Audit diagram
- o Cross-Functional Flowchart
- o Basic Flowchart
- o Basic Network Diagram
- o Gantt Chart

- o Timeline
- o Work Flow Diagram
- o Organization Chart Wizard
- o Floor plan
- o Schedule
- o Software and database
- o Engineering

However, the professional edition does include these templates.

- o Microsoft SharePoint Workflow
- o BPMN Diagram
- o Detailed Network Diagram
- o UML Sequence
- o UML Use Case
- o UML Class
- o Value Stream Map

To utilize the starter diagram

- Select any of the thumbnails from the template.
- Select one of the following actions in the template information panel:
  - o Double-click on the desired starter diagram thumbnail.
  - o Click on the thumbnail of the desired starter diagram, then choose "Create."

To remove the tips pane of a starter diagram

Do one of the following:

- o Press the Erase key after clicking anywhere inside the tips window.
- o Right-click on the tips pane and then click Cut.

Navigate Through the Drawing Window

Upon opening a document in Visio, you'll notice two windows beneath the ribbon. The Shapes window houses one or more stencils, each represented by a header bar containing the stencil's name. When dragging the pointer within the Shapes window, a scroll bar may appear to the right of the headers, depending on the number of open stencils. The Shapes window will be further discussed in the following section.

The larger window on the right, known as the drawing window, contains the drawing page. Surrounding the drawing window on the top and left are rulers displaying measurements in inches, millimeters, or other chosen units, as determined by either your selection or the template's settings. The gray area between the drawing page and the ruler is referred to as the canvas. Shapes placed on this canvas are visible in the drawing window but will not be printed.

Next, you'll find a few page controls located at the bottom left of the drawing window. Below are the functions they offer.

- ▪ **Page Name Tabs**: These tabs display the names of each page, with the active page's name appearing in a distinct color. Click on any tab to select your desired page. Right-click on any page name tab to access various page management functions, including the Duplicate Page option.

- **Insert page (+) button**: You can select a new page by choosing this option. Below the shapes and drawings, you'll find a status bar equipped with various indicators, controls, and buttons. The details displayed on the left side of the status bar may vary depending on the context. When nothing is selected on the drawing page, the left side of the status bar will resemble the image below.

PAGE 3 OF 3   ENGLISH (UNITED STATES)

- **Page Number**: The active page displays all pages within the current drawing. Click on this button to access the Page dialog box.
- **Language**: In this section, you will find the language in which the current drawing is written. The language settings are determined by the language setting on your Windows PC or Visio.
- **Macros**: Choosing "Macros" will initiate the Macros. Upon selecting a shape from the drawing page, you will observe the left side of the status bar as demonstrated here.

PAGE 3 OF 3   WIDTH: 1.5 IN.   HEIGHT: 1.5 IN.   ANGLE 0°   ENGLISH (UNITED STATES)

The width and height buttons display the dimensions of the selected shape, while the angle button indicates the rotation angle. Clicking any of these buttons will open the Size & Position window.

The right side of the status bar also features several buttons and controls that influence how you view the diagram.

- **Presentation Mode**: Selecting this view option will display the diagram in full-screen presentation mode.
- **Zoom slider**: Adjusting this slider allows you to zoom in or out on the diagram.
- **Zoom level button**: This indicates the current zoom level. Selecting it will open the dialog box where you can adjust zoom settings.
- **Fit Page to Current Window**: Select one of these options to resize the drawing page in order to view the entire page, if desired.
- **Switch the windows**: This button allows you to switch between windows in Visio.

Right-clicking anywhere in the status bar will bring up the Customize Status Bar menu. From this menu, you can choose to enable or disable the display of any of the buttons and controls on the status bar.

Click here to view a list of all pages in the diagram

- Choose one of the following options:
  o Click the All-Pages button located to the right of the last visible page name pane.

  o Click the Page Number button positioned at the far-left end of the status bar.

Click here to navigate to another page

- Choose one of the following options:
  o Select the desired page by clicking its name tab.
  o Choose the name of the desired page from the list of all pages.

To navigate between windows, perform one of the following actions:

- o Navigate to the right side of the status bar and select "**Switch Windows**."
- o Access the View tab, enter the Window group, and then select the "**Switch Windows**" button. From there, choose the window name you wish to open instead.

Move Between the Page Name Tabs

Prior to Visio 2013, navigating among the pages of your diagram was facilitated by four-page navigation buttons located in the lower-left corner of the drawing window. Two buttons allowed scrolling of the page name tabs left and right, while the other two buttons allowed jumping to the first or last page. These navigation buttons proved useful, particularly when the number of pages or the length of the page titles resulted in some page names being obscured.

While those controls are no longer available as of Visio 2016, you can still scroll through pages from left to right using an unseen button. To access it, click in the space directly to the left of the first visible page name tab.

Additionally, you can scroll pages differently by clicking the right-most visible page name tab.

Unfortunately, there are no buttons available for quick navigation to the first or last page. However, you can utilize the techniques outlined in the procedures mentioned in the preceding topic to navigate to any specific page, regardless of whether its name tab is visible. For instance, selecting "All pages" will display the results in a list.

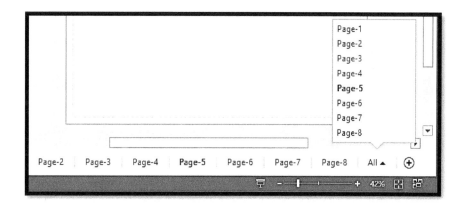

Below is the keyboard shortcut for switching between pages.

Ctrl+ Page down: This command moves you one page to the right.

Ctrl+ page up: This command moves you one page to the left.

Manage the shapes window

As depicted in the image above, the top section of the Shapes window features the title bars of all open stencils, while the lower part displays shapes from the currently selected stencil. Clicking the title bar of any open stencil allows you to switch to it. When a stencil's title bar is clicked, the title bars remain fixed, and the stencil always opens in the precise location beneath all title bars. This represents a significant improvement over Visio versions preceding Visio 2010.

The Shapes window is typically anchored to the left of the drawing window and showcases one or two columns of masters. However, depending on the diagram you're creating or revising, you may want to customize or relocate the Shapes window.

You can use the arrow buttons to collapse or expand the Shapes window. In the example below, the minimize button is located on the left, while the expand button is on the right. Collapsing the Shapes window is particularly useful when the symbols representing the masters in the stencil are easily recognizable.

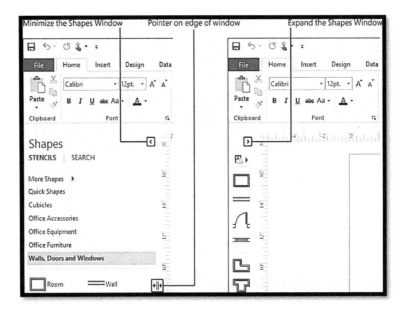

Afterward, you can choose to undock and float the Shapes window if you wish to reposition it within the Visio window. Alternatively, you can also close the window if needed.

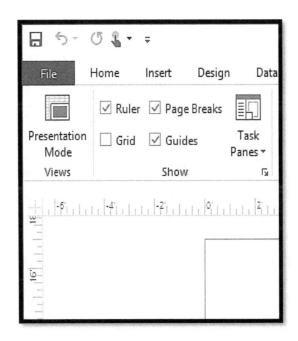

You can adjust the width of the Shapes window by sliding its right edge, changing one column at a time. However, locating the right edge is no longer as straightforward as it used to be. An interface enhancement introduced in Visio 2013 causes window boundaries to blend into the background, minimizing visual interference with the drawing's content. Consequently, when the Shapes window is docked on the left, the right side remains hidden unless the pointer is directly above it.

To enhance visibility of the boundary, gently move the pointer across the right side of the window until it switches to the window resize tool. You will be able to observe the resize tool within the left image. Due to the user interface update, navigation bars in smaller windows are only visible when the cursor is inside the window. Similarly, the scroll bar appears when the cursor is within the window, as depicted in the picture on the right. This presents an issue in the Shapes window because you cannot determine if there are additional masters below the bottom boundary of the window without pointing to them. In the image on the left, other furniture shapes are not visible.

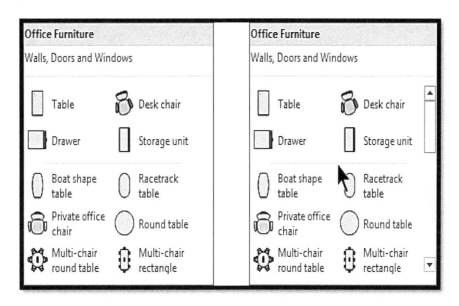

You can utilize various stencils from different templates. Additionally, you have the flexibility to switch between different stencils simultaneously.

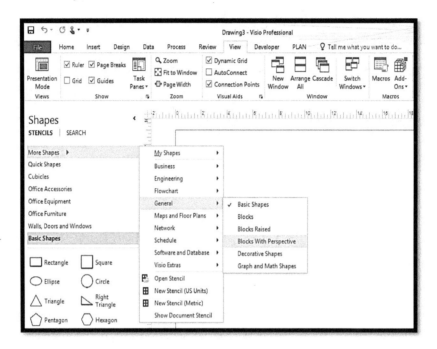

To Exit the Shapes Window

- Select the "**Minimize Shapes Window**" option.

    o To open the Shapes window, click the "**+**" button.

    o Click on the Shapes Window button to expand it.

- Adjust the size of the Shapes window by sliding the pointer along the right side of the window until it changes into a window resize tool.

- Move the window's border to the left or right.

To Eliminate the Shapes window from the dock

    o Drag the window's header onto the drawing page.

Docking the Shapes of the window

- o Position the window's header at one of the four edges of the main Visio window.

To show or hide the Shapes window

- o Navigate to the View tab, then within the Show group, click on the Task Panes button and select Shapes.

If you wish to open another stencil, follow these steps

- o Click on "More Shapes" in the Shapes window.
- o Select the desired template category name from the list.
- o Choose the stencil name you want from the list of stencil names.
- o Optionally, you can select another stencil either from the same template category you chose earlier or from a different one.
- o You can close the pop-up menu by clicking anywhere outside the stencil.

Pan and Zoom in the Drawing Window

When working with Visio diagrams, you frequently need to zoom in and out and pan (move left-right and up-down) within the drawing window. These actions can be accomplished using various methods, including mouse gestures, specific Pan & Zoom window controls, and keyboard shortcuts.

The quickest method to view a specific part of the page is by drawing a bounding box, which will result in the following.

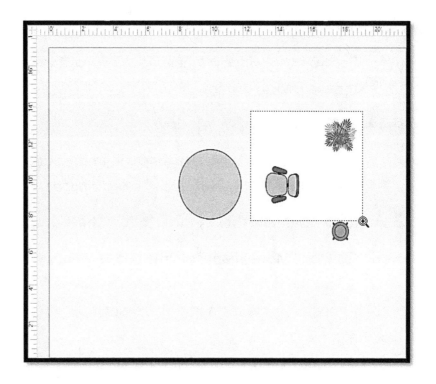

However, when you zoom, this is what you'll see.

Alternatively, you can draw the rectangle within the Pan and Zoom window. You can pan or zoom by dragging or resizing the rectangle inside the Pan and Zoom window.

The Pan & Zoom window may not be essential and can sometimes obstruct the design process. However, it proves useful when dealing with large drawing pages, such as engineering designs, floor plans, or office layouts.

The need to zoom in and out while working with a diagram is so prevalent that there are likely more methods, including keyboard shortcuts and mouse buttons, dedicated to this action compared to any other action in Visio.

To Show or Conceal the Pan & Zoom window

Go to the View tab, then in the Display group, click on Task Panes, and select **Pan** & **Zoom**.

To Magnify

Perform any of the following actions:

- Press and hold the Shift and Ctrl buttons while clicking the left mouse button.
- While continuing to hold the Shift and Ctrl buttons, roll the mouse.
- Alternatively, press Alt+F6.
- Adjust the Zoom slider lever on the status bar.
- Click on the Zoom level icon on the status bar to select a zoom level.
- In the Zoom group on the View tab, click the Zoom button, then select your preferred zoom level.
- Access the Pan & Zoom window, then reposition it to draw a smaller rectangle than the one currently present.
- Open the Pan & Zoom window, then adjust the edges or corners of the selected rectangle to make it smaller.

To Adjust the Size of the Drawing page to fit the Current Window

Choose one of the following options:

- o Click on the "Fit page to the current window" button in the status bar.
- o In the Zoom group on the View tab, click on the "Fit to Window" button.

To Rotate the Diagram

You can carry out any of these steps:

- o Rotate the mouse wheel (pans up and down).
- o Hold down the Shift key while rolling the mouse wheel (pans left and right).
- o Click and drag with the right mouse button while holding the Shift and Ctrl buttons.
- o Drag the selected rectangle within the Pan & Zoom window.

Summary

As you can observe, there are numerous actions you can perform with Visio. In this chapter, we covered some fundamental aspects that you need to be familiar with right after starting the Visio software. But wait, that's not all! Hold your horses. We'll delve deeper into the topics introduced in this chapter in the subsequent chapters.

CHAPTER 2

Create Diagrams

Creating a diagram from scratch might not always be straightforward. Therefore, Visio provides a wide range of templates for different types of diagrams. In the Standard edition, there are twenty templates divided into six categories, while in the Professional edition, there are over seventy templates organized into eight categories.

Every template consists of one or more stencils, each containing a variety of shapes suitable for the specific diagram type. Regardless of the template chosen, the ability to position and edit shapes is essential. While some shapes possess formulas that provide them with intricate behaviors, others are straightforward. Throughout this and subsequent chapters, you will encounter examples of both simple shapes and intelligent forms.

Position shapes utilizing the Dynamic Grid

The purpose of the Dynamic Grid is to simplify the precise placement or sizing of a shape when you drop it onto a page or move it, minimizing the need to manually adjust the shape afterwards. The enhanced Dynamic Grid in Visio 2021 offers more visual feedback compared to previous versions of the product.

The Dynamic Grid indicates when the circle aligns with the top, middle, and bottom of the rectangle. It assists in shape alignment by displaying vertical or horizontal dashed lines. To understand how this functions.

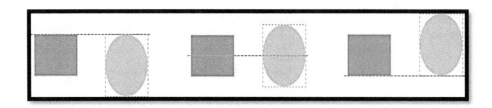

Within the dynamic grid, you'll also notice a double-headed arrow with varying lengths, aiding in spacing the shape and adjusting its size.

In this scenario, you'll observe a double-headed arrow

You'll notice a double-headed arrow within the interval between shapes, which matches the preset spacing for that page.

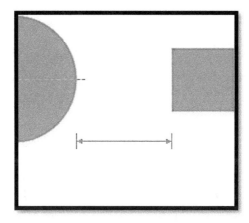

Your new shape perfectly fits into an existing space, and likewise for the other shape on the page.

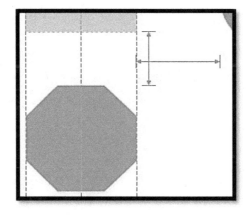

When resizing a shape, you'll also observe the double-headed arrow, ensuring its dimensions align with one or more shapes already present on the page.

It's worth noting that you can adjust the standard inter-shape space for any page, as the double arrows represent the default space for a page.

By default, the dialog box settings align both vertical and horizontal intervals. You can adjust the vertical interval individually by unchecking the "Use Similar Spacing for Both" checkboxes.

All the shapes above were created using the basic shapes stencils that are automatically available when you use the basic diagram template. However, the dynamic grid function also applies to shapes created using drawing tools found within the Tools group on the Home tab. For added convenience, you can access the drawing tools in the upper left corner of the mini toolbar.

While the Dynamic Grid was beneficial prior to Visio 2013, its utility has been enhanced significantly since then. It now responds more swiftly to pointer movement and shape positions and provides more comprehensive visual feedback. Additionally, since the backdrop page grid has been disabled by default in Visio 2016 and Visio 2013, the Dynamic Grid has become particularly crucial for aligning shapes in these versions of the software.

If you don't see the dynamic grid lines when moving shapes near others already on the page, it may be because the feature is turned off for the drawing. You can activate the grid lines by checking the "Dynamic Grid" checkbox within the Visual Aids group under the View tab.

Inserting Shapes onto a Page

Drag a shape from a stencil onto the drawing canvas to place it there.

Aligning Shapes with the Dynamic Grid

Position a shape adjacent to the top, bottom, or either side of an existing shape, then wait for the Dynamic Grid lines to appear.

Aligning Shapes on Both Axes with the Dynamic Grid

Position a shape to the left or right of another shape, and observe the Dynamic Grid lines appearing in both the horizontal and vertical directions.

Spacing shapes utilizing the Dynamic Grid

Select one of the following choices

- o Gently move a shape left or right until a double-headed arrow appears by dragging it beside another shape.
- o Drag a shape over or under another shape, then gradually raise or lower it until a double-headed arrow appears.

To adjust the default inter-shape spacing on a page

- o Access the Spacing Options dialog box by choosing "**Position**" in the Arrange group of the Home tab, then selecting "**Spacing Options**."

- o If you want to set different spacing intervals for the horizontal and vertical dimensions, uncheck the "Use identical spacing for both" checkboxes in the Spacing Settings dialog box.
- o Select your desired spacing by adjusting the Horizontal interval or either the Horizontal or Vertical spacing, then click **OK**.

How to Use Drawing Tools to Construct Shapes

Right-click anywhere on the drawing page, then choose Drawing Tools from the context menu, and select a tool.

Or

Click on the drawing tools icon located under the Tools group on the Home tab, and then select a tool.

Drag to Create a Shape

How to create a square using the sketching tools

- o   Select the Rectangle tool.
- o   While dragging, hold down the Shift key.

How to Create a Circle Using the Sketching Tools

- o   First, select the Ellipse tool.
- o   While dragging, hold down the Shift key.

To align the size and shapes created using the drawing tools, you'll need to reposition and resize them in the same manner as shapes created using stencils.

Choose shapes

In Visio, there are several methods to select shapes, including clicking on individual shapes, using Area Select, and Lasso Select. Additionally, you can select all shapes on a page and then add a shape to the current selection.

In Visio, clicking and dragging on a drawing page typically triggers area selection by default. Only shapes within the gray bounding box are selected unless you adjust the Visio selection settings. For example, upon releasing the mouse button, the rectangles and octagons on the left side of the image will be selected, while no shapes will be selected on the right side.

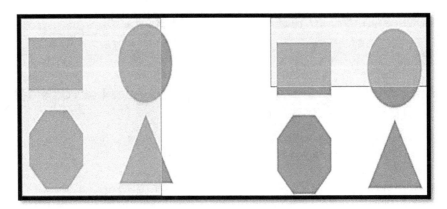

The less commonly used Lasso Select method provides greater flexibility, allowing you to encircle desired shapes with a freeform line. Similar to a bounding box, Visio typically selects only fully enclosed shapes when the mouse button is released. In the image on the right side, only the octagon and circle are selected using the lasso tool.

To alter the selection behavior in Visio to include shapes partially enclosed by a bounding box or lasso, follow these steps: Navigate to the File tab to access the Backstage view, then select Options followed by Advanced in the left pane. Finally, check the box labeled Pick Shapes Partly Inside Area.

When employing Lasso Select, release the mouse button just before the "rope" commences to ensure the desired shapes are selected. It's preferable to conclude your selection where you initiated it, although it's not mandatory. In certain situations, a partially closed loop will still select some shapes.

Selecting a Single Shape

Click once on the shape.

How to Select Multiple Shapes with a Single Click

- o   Select the first shape by clicking once.
- o   While selecting additional shapes, hold down the Shift or Ctrl keys.

Area Select allows you to select one or more shapes

To create a bounding box around the shape or shapes you want, click once on the drawing page and drag.

To Toggle between Lasso Select and Area Select

Click the Select button in the Editing group of the Home tab, then choose Lasso Select.

Click on "Lasso" for Lasso Selection

While holding down the mouse button, draw a lasso around the desired shape or shapes, and release the mouse button close to where you started.

Going back to the Utilization of Bounding boxes

Click on the Select button to choose the area you want to select

To combine a click selection with an area or lasso selection:

Perform one of the following actions:

- o   Select one or more shapes, and then add additional shapes by either dragging a bounding box or lasso selection while holding down the **Shift** or **Ctrl keys**.
- o   Alternatively, start by creating a bounding box or lasso selection, and then add more shapes by clicking on them while holding down the **Shift** or **Ctrl keys**.

Removing Shapes from a Selection:

To remove shapes from the selection, hold down the Shift or Ctrl keys while clicking on the shapes.

To Select Every Shape on a Page:

Press Ctrl+A.

To Copy, Paste and Duplicate shapes

Visio 2016 and newer versions operate more efficiently compared to their immediate predecessors. In versions prior to 2010, Visio would automatically paste shapes into the center of the drawing window, which could sometimes be desirable but often required additional dragging and adjustments.

Visio will replicate the positioning of a shape or multiple shapes from Page 1 onto Page 2, regardless of whether that specific area of the page is visible when pasting. This occurs when copying shapes from Page 1 and pasting them onto Page 2.

When pasting shapes onto the same page from which they were copied, the process operates slightly differently:

- o If the copied shapes are still visible within the drawing window after pasting, the pasted shapes will be positioned with a slight offset beneath and to the side of the original shapes.
- o If the copied shapes are not currently displayed within the drawing window, Visio will paste them into the center of the drawing window.

Shapes can be duplicated instead of copied and pasted. They can be pasted to the same spot on the same page or a different page.

Duplicated shapes are positioned slightly to the right and below the original shapes.

One advantage of duplicating shapes rather than copying them is that duplication doesn't involve the Clipboard. The original data remains on the Clipboard when you duplicate shapes.

Copying shapes

- After selecting the shapes you want to copy, press Ctrl+C.

To paste shapes into a page and allow Visio to determine their placement

Select one of the following options:

- To paste two or more copied shapes onto the same page, you can use the Ctrl+V keyboard shortcut. Visio will offset the pasted shapes slightly from the original shapes.
- Alternatively, you can use Ctrl+V to paste the shapes after scrolling until the original shapes are no longer visible on the screen. In this case, Visio will center them in the drawing window.

Also, it's important to note that if Auto Size is enabled, Visio may expand the size of the drawing page to accommodate the pasted shapes. If Auto Size is not enabled, the pasted shape will be inserted onto the canvas as it is.

How to Duplicate Shapes to a Different page and let Visio

determine their placement

- Make a copy of two or more shapes first.
- Select the tab labeled "Page Name" located at the bottom of the drawing window to switch to a new page.

Or

- o To include a page in the diagram, select the Insert Page button (represented by the plus sign).
- o Press Ctrl+V to transfer the copied shapes onto the paper. See how exactly where they were on the first page transfers to the next one in Visio?

Pasting shapes onto a page to add them

- o Right-click on the desired page where you want to paste the copied shapes.

- o Select "Paste" from the context menu.

To copy a specific shape or multiple shapes

Select one of the following actions:

- o Press Ctrl+D.
- o Drag the shapes while holding down the Ctrl key, then click and hold the mouse button until they are in the desired location.

Arrange Shapes Using Rulers and Guides

As discussed earlier in this chapter, while the Visio Dynamic Grid feature offers alignment capabilities, it may not always suffice for your requirements. For instance, if there are shapes positioned between the ones you're trying to align, the Dynamic Grid won't be effective. There might be scenarios where you need to align shapes in a manner not supported by the Dynamic Grid.

Utilize Rulers for Aligning and Sizing Shapes

You can utilize the ruler to adjust positions and sizes. One ruler is situated along the left edge of the drawing window, while another is located at the top. In diagrams created with the US template, the ruler displays measurements in feet and inches. Conversely, if metric units are employed, the ruler will show measurements in meters, centimeters, or millimeters.

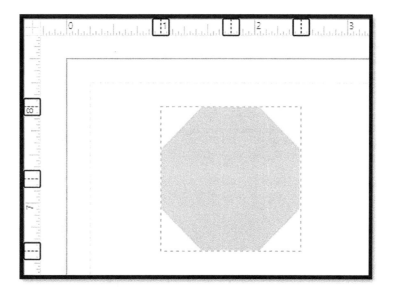

As you move objects on the drawing page in Visio, the ruler provides visual position indicators with dashed lines. In the example below, the dashed lines on the top ruler denote the top, middle, and bottom of the octagon, while those on the side ruler indicate its left, right, and center. You can utilize the arrows on the rulers to precisely position the shapes as you move them.

When resizing a shape by dragging a side handle horizontally or vertically, a dashed line appears on the corresponding ruler. Similarly, when adjusting the shape's size in both dimensions by dragging a corner handle, a dashed line appears on each ruler.

Utilize Guides for Aligning and Sizing Shapes

Guides not only aid in aligning objects but also facilitate moving groups of aligned shapes together. To create guides, simply click on a ruler and drag it onto the drawing page. You can add as many horizontal or vertical guides as needed to your page.

While guides are helpful in many scenarios, they are particularly valuable in situations like the one depicted below. Because of the horizontal rectangle positioned between the stars in this diagram, the Dynamic Grid cannot be used to align them. Consequently, a vertical line has been added to the page to assist in alignment.

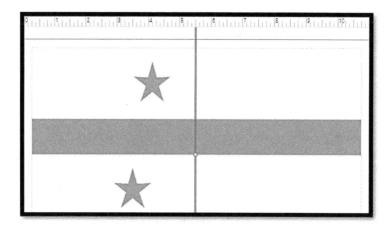

If guides are not visible on the page or you wish to hide them, navigate to the View tab and access the Show group, then select or deselect the Guides checkbox. Additionally, you can align a shape to the center or the side by moving it towards the guide.

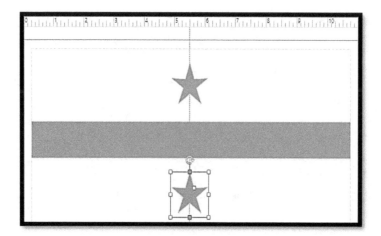

It's crucial to note that the stars are firmly aligned with the guide. If the guide is moved, the stars will adjust accordingly. However, if the guide is no longer needed, you can delete it like any other shape, thus allowing individual alignment adjustments without affecting all aligned shapes collectively.

Using a Guide to Align Shapes is a Straightforward Process:

- o **Create a Guide:** Click on a ruler (either horizontal or vertical) and drag it onto the drawing page to create a guide. You can create as many guides as needed for alignment purposes.
- o **Align Shapes:** Once the guide is in place, you can move shapes towards it to align them. Shapes can be dragged and aligned with the guide to ensure precise positioning.
- o **Adjust as Needed:** If adjustments are required, you can move the guide or shapes accordingly. Guides provide a visual reference for alignment, making it easier to ensure that shapes are properly positioned relative to each other.
- o **Hide or Delete Guides:** If guides are no longer needed or if they clutter the workspace, you can hide or delete them. Simply go to the View tab, navigate to the Show group, and toggle the Guides checkbox to hide or show guides. To delete a guide, select it and press the delete key or right-click and choose delete.

Shifting Shapes Adhesive-to-a-Guide

- Adhere two or more forms to a guide employing the method described above.
- Observe how all aligned forms follow the guidance by moving it to a new location.

Eliminating a Guide

Choose the guide and press the delete button.

Change a Shape's size, Reposition and Orientation

Drawn shapes on the drawing page might need to be resized or relocated, and Visio provides a number of ways to accomplish this. You are able to employ the mouse, keyboard, or both to make changes to the shape; you can also utilize the Size & Location panel. You can open the Basic Flowchart template from the Flowchart template group, and it will display the Basic Flowchart Shapes stencil. It includes the forms shown in the pictures in this session.

Utilize Control Handles

A group of white squares known as the handles will appear once you select a form.

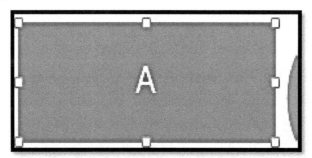

- You may change the shape's height or breadth by moving the square handles located in the center of each edge.
- • By adjusting the square handles on the corners, the width and height can be changed proportionally.

There may be times when you have problems dragging one or more handles on a form. By default, this indicates that any form features have been locked by the shape developer. A locked shape's height is shown by diagonal slashes in Shape B's top and bottom handles on the right side of the image. Also, notice the cuts that cross the corner handles. If you are unable to adjust the height, using a corner handle will not allow you to change both dimensions simultaneously. Locked handles in Visio had a different color than unlocked handles in previous versions of the program. More recently released Visio versions have more subdued differentiation, which is based on the diagonal lines that are described alongside the picture.

A circular arrow is displayed in addition to the side and corner handles at the top center of the most selected forms. Right side of the image is where you can see the rotation handle. Turning the form about its pin requires clicking and dragging the rotation handle. There is no visibility of the left rotation handle since Shape A has locked the rotation. You may change how accurate the shape rotation is by altering the distance between the rotation handle and the pointer.

For example, if the pointer is in close proximity to the rotation handle, the item will rotate in 15-degree steps. You can only move the object a fraction of a degree at a time as you pull the pointer out of the object, which rotates in ever-smaller steps. You may view the incremental rotation angle progress as you turn an object using the Size & Position window.

Control handles are a tool used by form designers to provide the user with control over different shape aspects. You can adjust the shape's size, text position within the shape, inner and outer line positions, and many other features by dragging and dropping control handles. As shown in the form **D** photos, for example, you can use the control handles to drag the inside vertical lines of the shape in the figure below. Together with rotating and scaling handles, some Visio shapes may additionally feature a yellow control handle.

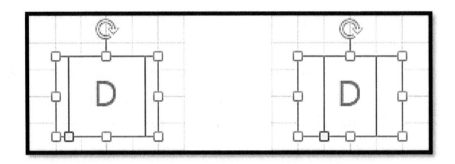

There are several forms with yellow control knobs when using Visio stencils. Play around with the yellow handle whenever you select a shape to discover how you may use it to alter its appearance. Ctrl+Z can be used to undo any changes you have made that you don't like.

Modify the Shape, Width and Height

A shape can be resized by selecting it and dragging it across the corner handles and side.

When you drag a resizing handle to adjust a form's width or height, look for a dashed line on the relevant ruler located close at the side of the drawing window.

The margin of the shape's position is indicated by the dotted line. After selecting a shape, you can rotate it by dragging the rotation handle. Drag the cursor across the screen as you approach closer and farther away from the object to watch the variations in the rotation increment.

Utilize the Size and Position window

The Size & Position window in Visio serves two purposes: it allows you to view and adjust the values of the six shape characteristics—X, Y, width, height, angle, and pin position—for two-dimensional shapes.

The size of the left-hand form in the illustration below is displayed as two inches wide in the Size & Position window. Entering 3.5 in the Width cell will immediately modify the object's width to 3.5 inches. In the event when a shape's age Y point is 50 mm and you enter 125 in the Y cell, the shape will advance to the new location on the page.

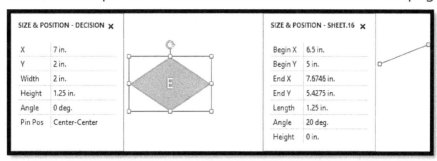

One-dimensional Visio forms display properties appropriate for a line in the Size & Position window, including the length and start/stop coordinates, as seen on the right in the image below.

If you insert a value into a Size & Position window cell without including units, Visio will automatically use the previous displayed values for that cell. It is possible to establish units when you enter values, though. For example, if the Y value is 60 mm and you enter 12 cm or 12 centimeters, Visio will translate and apply the value, resulting in a display of 120 mm.

Even between various measurement systems, Visio can translate. In the example above, if you enter 3 in or 3 inches, Visio will modify the shape and show the outcome as 76.2 mm.

The function of the first five rows of the Size & Position window for two-dimensional forms is quite evident; however, the sixth row requires some explanation. Most shapes have a default Pin Pos of Center-Center, which rotates the object around its center, as seen in the picture below. Pin position, or simply Pin Pos, is the center of rotation for a form. Altering the pin positions allows you to rotate the form around a different point.

Any changes you make to a shape's Pin Pos will affect where the shape appears on the page. The location of the pin inside the shape will determine where it appears on the page. This is so that the pin genuinely describes where the shape's X and Y coordinates should be put, instead than the shape's center coordinates.

The two features of a line or the three properties of a two-dimensional shape can also be seen without opening the Size & Position box. Visio shows two or three of the chosen shape's attributes on the status bar at the bottom of the Visio window.

Page 1 of 1	Length: 2.5 in.	Angle: 20°	English (United States)	
Page 1 of 1	Width: 2 in.	Height: 1.25 in.	Angle: 40°	English (United States)

The image above on the bottom depicts a two-dimensional shape, whereas the image above displays a line.

Select one of the options below to view the Size & Position window

- Select the Show group's Task Panes by clicking on the View tab, and then select Size & Position.
- Click a button from the status bar (Length, Width, Height, or Angle) once a shape has been selected.

To view the modifications to Shape Properties

1. Select a shape.
2. Open the (optional) Size & Position window.
3. Move the shape around the page by dragging it.

   Or

You can use the resize handles to change the shape's height and width.

4. Once you've made any necessary adjustments in the previous step, notice the new figures on the Visio status bar or open the Size & Position window.

Changing the Properties of the Shape Utilizing the size and Position Window

1. Select a shape and then open the Size & Position window.
2. Adjust any shape property and see how the form changes as a result.

Utilizing the Lines to Combine shapes

Visio provides one-dimensional (1-D) and two-dimensional (2-D) forms (2-D). Forms in one dimension operate similarly to lines having joinable ends. Two-dimensional shapes act like polygons with interiors and edges.

A few forms in Visio appear two-dimensional but are actually one-dimensional; examples include those found under the headings "Add equipment to rack diagrams" and "Build network and data center diagrams." The converse is also occasionally true.

Among the six tools accessible through the drawing tools button, situated adjacent to the Pointer Tools in the Tools group on the Home tab, lies the Line tool.

In Visio, one way to draw a line is to use the Line tool. Whenever the cursor is above the drawing tools button on the left side of the screen, the active drawing tool is highlighted in the ScreenTip.

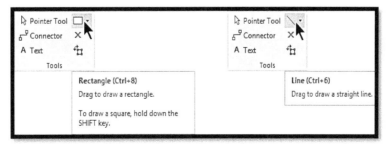

If you would want to use the line tool but it is not available, pick the arrow that appears after the tool that is displayed on the button. Next, select the tool that you desire. When you select the Line tool, the outcome will be displayed on the right.

The little toolbar also gives you access to the drawing tools, as seen in the image above. With this approach, the cursor returns to the Pointer Tool after drawing one line with the Line tool.

When you pick the Line tool, the cursor changes to a plus sign with a diagonal line to its bottom right, as you can see in the left graphic of the picture below. Many dark gray squares, sometimes referred to as connecting points, are depicted in the same figure on the left. When you move the Line tool near a shape in Visio 2016, connection points on the shape become apparent.

Some shapes lack connection points. When employing the Line tool and encountering a shape without visible gray squares, it suggests the absence of connection points within that shape.

Alternatively, the shape might indeed possess connection points, but they may be hidden due to the global setting to display connection points being turned off. To verify this, check the Connection Points checkbox within the Visual Aids group on the View tab to confirm whether connection point visibility is enabled or disabled.

By bringing the Line tool sufficiently close, a green square emerges around a connection point, as depicted in the illustration located to the right in the preceding image. Clicking on the connecting point secures the line to the shape.

In the image on the left, a line is attached at both ends and remains selected. The left end of the line, where it was initially attached, displays a visible green circle. Conversely, the "to" end, indicating the destination, exhibits a white circle with a small green dot at its center. The starting end of a line is commonly referred to as the "from" end.

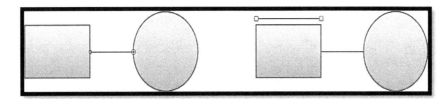

Within this image, the line positioned above the rectangle lacks adherence to any shape. Notably, the "to" end of this line features a gray square, while the "from" end exhibits a white square. Visio underscores the color contrast between the attached and unattached line ends in the image, facilitating clear differentiation. While this instance showcases a straightforward visual indication of connection, subsequent examples illustrate how the color of line ends can also denote connectivity.

Placing a line end inside a shape or on its edge won't result in adhesion if you attempt to glue it to a shape lacking connection points. In the forthcoming illustration, an observation awaits. The "from" end of the line is affixed to the center of the octagon, whereas the "to" end, positioned near the edge of the elongated rectangle, remains unattached, denoted by the presence of a gray square.

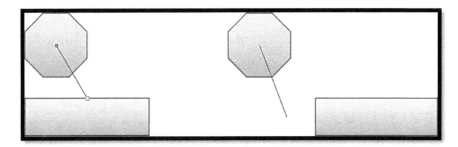

To determine whether the line remains unattached, simply move the rectangle.

There are four tools available for drawing lines, namely:

- o Using line tools, create a straight line
- o The arc tool is used to draw an arc
- o The freeform tool is used to draw lines with many bends; and
- o The pencil tool is used to draw straight or curved lines. But you may also use it to reshape or alter already-existing 1D or 2D shapes.

Keeping their shape when the shapes they have adhered to are moved is an important characteristic of the four-line sorts. Whether a line stays straight or squiggly depends on its starting shape; if it starts straight, it will stay that way. The dynamic connector, covered in the item that follows, stands in stark contrast to this behavior.

This is the way the Line, Freeform, Arc or Pencil tool is used

- o To select the desired tool, hit the drawing tools button located in the Tools group on the Home tab.

Or

Hit the Drawing Tools button after performing a right-click on the drawing page. From the small toolbar, locate the tool of your choice by clicking on it.

Drag it to Create a Line

These are the steps to attach a line to a shape

- ▪ Select the line tool that you want. When the pointer approaches a shape, the connecting points will show.
- ▪ Move the cursor in the vicinity of a shape until the connection point is visible.
- ▪ After choosing a connection point, drag the opposite end of the line to another connection point on the same or different shape.

Select the Pointer Tool button once you've selected any line tools from the Home page.

Select one option from the list below

- From the Tools group, select the Pointer Tool icon.
- Press Ctrl+1.

Sidebar: Make 2-D shapes Utilizing Line Tools

The array of line drawing tools serves more than just sketching one-dimensional shapes. With these tools, you can create a flawless line that maintains a constant direction or connect segments to form intricate designs. Simply closing the loop where you began can transform your creation into a two-dimensional object.

Merge the Shapes Utilizing Dynamic Connection Points

Within the 1-D shapes covered in the previous segment, bends, curves, and corners are possible, but only if you consciously add them or employ a tool. When you use Visio to add or delete corners or curves to 1-D objects, you can create dynamic connectors, also known as connectors, which adjust their geometry relative to other shapes.

Dynamic connectors play a vital role in various linked diagrams, allowing you to precisely position two-dimensional shapes. Meanwhile, Visio efficiently manages one-dimensional shapes, freeing you to arrange the two-dimensional shapes for diagrams like flowcharts, organization charts, and network diagrams. While there may arise occasions when you need to intervene or adjust Visio's settings, often allowing Visio to handle dynamic connector placement and routing proves effective.

In addition to the plethora of line tools available, there exist various methods through which you can opt to utilize a dynamic connector:

- Choose the Connector tool from the Tools group on the Home tab. Once activated, this tool remains selected until you opt for a different one.
- Right-click on the drawing sheet or a shape, then select the Add One Connection to the Page button. This method allows you to draw a single connector using the small toolbar before reverting to the Pointer Tool.
- Utilize the AutoConnect feature, discussed in detail in the section "Using AutoConnect and Quick Shapes" later in this chapter.

Additionally, you have the option to establish a connection with a shape using its connection points

Upon activating the connector tool, you'll notice the pointer transforming into a black arrow, accompanied by arrows featuring two right-angle bends beneath it. Just like the line tools discussed earlier, when you bring the connector tool near a specific connection point, a green square will encircle the connection point. Refer to the illustration on the right side of the figure for visual guidance.

Clicking on a connecting point permanently attaches the line to it. Subsequently, you establish a static bond between two connecting sites by dragging the line to a different connection point and releasing the mouse button. Regardless of how the connected shapes are moved, the connector remains fixed at the same two positions. Pay attention to the arrowhead located at the "to" end of the connector in the illustration on the left. While the green handles in this illustration often obscure the arrowhead, it becomes visible whenever the dynamic connector is deselected, as shown on the right-hand side of the figure. While dynamic connections frequently feature arrowheads and other line ends by default, each one-dimensional shape can possess them.

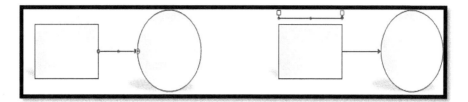

Moving to the right side, you'll notice a connector positioned atop a rectangle, not yet adhered to any specific shape. At the "from" end of the connector, there's a white square, while the "to" end displays a gray square. Remarkably, the connector remains intelligent, irrespective of whether it's drawn straight. This inherent adaptability distinguishes the dynamic connector as a standout feature.

Utilizing the Connector Tool

- To access the Connector tool, simply navigate to the Tools group located on the Home tab and select it from there.

Or

To opt for a one-time-use Connector tool, right-click on the drawing page, and then choose the "Add One Connector to the Page" button located within the lower-left corner of the mini toolbar.

- Drag to establish a dynamic connection.

Attaching a connection point to a dynamic connector using static adhesive (glue)

- Select the tool for a permanent Connector.
- Opt for the connector tool for single use.
- Drag it to the next point after clicking on a connection point.

Connect to Shapes without Connection Spots

The behavior differs significantly when you drag an unglued dynamic connector end towards a shape lacking connection points compared to dragging a line end towards the same shape. In the image, the "from" end of the connector has been attached to a connection point directly in the center of the octagon. However, if you drag the opposite end of the connector to a correct angle with no connection point, the border of the shape will shift to light green.

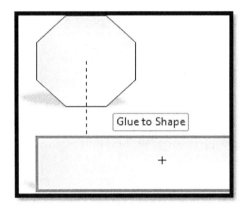

Also, observe the pointer's position within the wide rectangle. In this alternate image, you'll observe that the "to" end of the arrow is connected to another location. Here, Visio employs dynamic glue on the rectangle, and the contact point is directly beneath the center of the octagon.

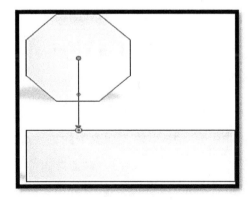

It's important to keep in mind that shapes with connection points react to the approach of a dynamic connector in much the same way as shapes without connection points. Consequently, there are two methods to connect a connector to a shape with connection points. By hovering over an area of the shape lacking connection points and then releasing the mouse button, you can either establish static adhesive to a specific connection point or dynamic adhesive to the shape as a whole.

To fully grasp the dynamic connector's capabilities, try moving one shape at either end and observe how Visio automatically adds or removes bends or corners. Understanding the distinctions between statically attached and dynamically glued dynamic connectors is also essential. Visio adjusts a dynamically glued connector to accommodate changes in the positions of one or both shapes at its ends. We will utilize the image below to illustrate this concept.

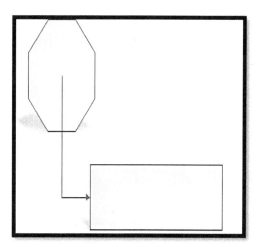

The rectangle has been shifted to the right from its initial position, causing the connector to make contact with another point on the corner.

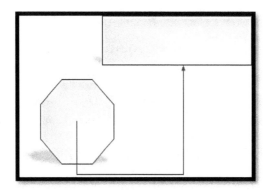

Next, on the right-hand side, the rectangle has been relocated to a spot on the octagon. Consequently, the connector becomes affixed to the bottom of the rectangle. Given that the connector has been glued to the center of the octagon, its position remains unchanged even as you move the shape.

Now, consider a scenario where both connectors utilize static glue. Regardless of the positions of the rectangle and the circle, the connector consistently exits the rectangle on the right side and enters the circle on the left.

Attach a dynamic connector to a shape using adhesive (dynamic glue)

- Select the tool for a permanent Connector.

Or

Opt for the connector tool for single use.

- Drag from any section of one shape to another without a connecting point by clicking any unconnected element of the first shape.

Adjust Connector Style and Segmentation

The default setting for the dynamic connector employs a right-angle bend, yet you have the flexibility to alter its visual presentation effortlessly. Simply right-click on the connector and select from one of three available options.

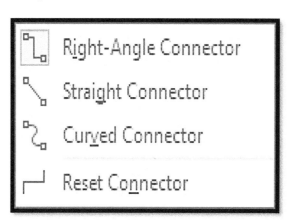

When shapes connected by dynamic connectors are moved in Visio, the connector segments are automatically adjusted. Additionally, selecting a connector reveals blue control handles at each bend and in the middle of each section, enabling you to physically reposition individual connector segments.

Should the dynamic connector become overly complex with numerous bends, you have the option to right-click on it and select "Reset Connector." Visio will then redraw the connector with minimal bends and segments necessary to accommodate the space requirements.

To Create a Bend in a Dynamic Connection

Select a shape to serve as the initial end of the dynamic connector. Then, relocate the shape to another position on the page.

To Move Segments of a Dynamic Connection

Step one involves selecting a dynamic connector with at least one bend. Next, slide one of the blue adjustment handles of the dynamic connector.

How to Adjust a Dynamic Connector's Appearance

- Select a dynamic connector containing at least one bend.
- Right-click on the connector to choose from the Right-Angle, Straight, or Curved Connector options.

To Revert a Dynamic Connection to its Simplest Configuration

Select the dynamic connector, then opt for "Reset Connector" from the context menu.

Sidebar: Recognizing 1-D Shapes and Varieties of Adhesive

In the preceding chapter, you explored various types of 1-D shapes along with two distinct types of adhesive.

This sidebar outlines the characteristics of 1-D shapes, including the visual indicators utilized by Visio to differentiate between connected and unconnected ends of 1-D shapes.

- When adjusting the shapes at their endpoints, a 1-D shape generated using any line tool (such as Line, Freeform, Arc, or Pencil) retains its initial form.
- The Connector tool introduces or removes bends in a line to accommodate the adjustment of a 1-D shape.
- Static adhesive is formed when a line or dynamic connector connects to a connection point; regardless of how the 2-D shape is repositioned, the 1-D shape remains linked at that stationary position.

- Dynamic adhesive is established when a dynamic connector connects to a shape without a connection point; as the 2-D shape moves, the attachment point of the dynamic connector adjusts accordingly.
- In this image, you'll find Image Square control handles. They're gray on the "to" end and white on the "from" end, forming a 1-D shape with unconnected ends. Check it out for yourself.

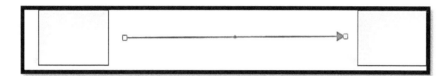

A one-dimensional shape with bonded endpoints is displayed using round control handles. At the "from" end, there's a green circle, while at the "to" end, there's a green dot enclosed within a white circle.

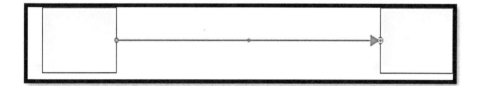

Utilize Auto connect and Quick Shapes

In Visio 2007, AutoConnect was introduced, providing a swift method to connect shapes with dynamic connectors. Building upon this feature, Visio 2010 introduced Quick Shapes, leveraging AutoConnect to enable even faster drawing production.

Employing the Dynamic Grid to align and space shapes as you place them on the page proves effective for numerous diagrams. However, for certain types of diagrams, utilizing Quick Shapes combinations offers an even superior option. Let's take a flow chart as the perfect example. When you bring a set of flow chart shapes onto the page in the desired configuration, you can effortlessly add a dynamic connector using the AutoConnect feature by simply pointing and clicking. Upon selecting a shape, the AutoConnect arrow will manifest as four small blue triangles.

If the AutoConnect arrow fails to appear when you interact with a shape, it's probable that AutoConnect is disabled for this design. To activate AutoConnect, navigate to the View tab, locate the Visual Aids category, and select the AutoConnect checkbox.

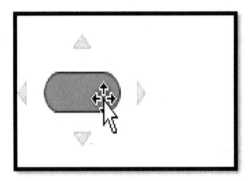

If the arrow still doesn't appear after adjusting the document settings, you have another option. Open the Visio Settings dialog box and select "**Advanced**." Ensure that the "**Allow AutoConnect**" checkbox is checked. You can access the Settings option in the Backstage view by clicking on it.

When you select one of the arrows, it activates a dynamic connector that spans the gap and dynamically attaches its end to both shapes. Introducing dynamic connectors to an existing shape is straightforward with AutoConnect. Each AutoConnect arrow scans for a nearby shape in the direction it points. But what if none of the four AutoConnect arrows align directly opposite each other? Well, AutoConnect simplifies this issue. You just need to drag an AutoConnect arrow onto any other shape to resolve it.

You might have noticed that AutoConnect arrows sometimes appear more promptly than at other times. If you've recently used AutoConnect and pause on a shape, the arrows emerge notably faster. However, if you haven't utilized AutoConnect recently, their appearance is delayed to avoid interrupting your workflow. Visio aims to provide them when you need them, hence the delay. Occasionally, you might observe that a shape only features AutoConnect arrows on certain sides. This occurs because the arrows appear only on the sides of shapes that aren't yet connected to surrounding shapes.

When using AutoConnect, you'll observe a live preview that offers a glimpse of the outcome when you briefly hover over an AutoConnect arrow before clicking, as demonstrated in the image below. Additionally, a small toolbar featuring four shapes is also displayed. While the Quick Shapes mini toolbar isn't useful for connecting existing shapes with AutoConnect, you'll discover in the subsequent sections of this chapter that it's advantageous for adding new shapes to the page.

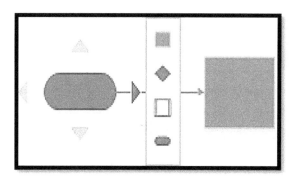

To access the Quick Shapes mini-toolbar, simply hover over the AutoConnect arrow adjacent to the start/end shape on the right. If you keep the pointer over the AutoConnect arrow, you'll see a live preview of the currently selected shape in the stencil.

With a single click, you can effortlessly add a second start/end shape to the existing drawing, and the new shape will automatically be positioned at the default distance for this page. However, if you prefer to add a different shape, Quick Shapes provide a convenient solution. In Visio 2016, you'll find a Quick Shapes area at the bottom of the stencils window pane for every open stencil, with most stencils featuring preselected Quick Shapes.

In the Shapes window, the Basic Flowchart Shapes feature a thin gray line that distinguishes the Document/Data shapes from the Database/External Data shapes. The initial four shapes displayed in the Quick Shapes section are the ones visible on the small toolbar. If you wish for different shapes to appear on the Quick Shapes mini-toolbar, simply drag them to occupy the first four positions in the Quick Shapes area of the stencil.

When you choose a shape from the Quick Shapes mini-toolbar, the live preview will automatically update to reflect the selected shape. Take a look at this illustration for reference.

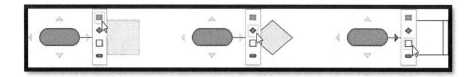

Start with a single shape on the page. Next, by clicking on "three" in the Quick Shapes mini-toolbar, you'll construct the diagram depicted in the image below.

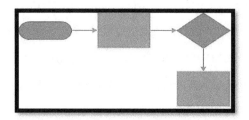

The preset spacing interval for the page dictates the placement of new shapes when you "**shoot**" them onto the drawing page using AutoConnect alone or in conjunction with Quick Shapes.

AutoConnect and Quick Shapes are invaluable tools when you require them. However, there are instances when they can get in the way. In such cases, remember that you can disable AutoConnect by unchecking it in the Visual Aids group on the View tab.

To Connect Adjacent Shapes Utilizing AutoConnect

- o Click on one of the shapes to prompt the AutoConnect arrows to appear when two shapes are adjacent on the drawing page but not connected.
- o Select the second shape by clicking on the AutoConnect arrow.

Utilizing AutoConnect to Connect Distant shapes

- o Click on one of the shapes until the AutoConnect arrow appears, indicating two shapes placed anywhere on the drawing page but not connected.
- o Position the other shape on top of a single AutoConnect arrow.

To Incorporate a shape from the stencils onto the page utilizing AutoConnect

- o Select the desired shape from the stencil.
- o Pick a shape on the drawing page by clicking one of the AutoConnect arrows.

The Procedure for Placing a Shape onto the Page Using

AutoConnect and Quick Shapes

- o To reveal the AutoConnect arrows, begin by hovering over a shape on the page.

- To display the Quick Shapes mini toolbar, hover over one of the AutoConnect arrows.
- Click on any shape in the mini toolbar to add it to the page.

The masters showcased on the Quick Shapes mini-toolbar can be customized

- Begin by opening a stencil containing more than four masters.
- Drag one of the masters to position it among the top four shapes above the quick shape line in the stencil.
- Confirm that the Quick Shapes mini-toolbar includes your master.

Utilize AutoAdd and Auto delete

With Visio, you can efficiently incorporate and remove shapes from a connected drawing, with Visio automatically adjusting the layout to accommodate the changes.

- When you utilize the AutoAdd feature to add a shape, Visio adapts the existing drawing layout to fit the new shape. This adjustment can range from minor to significant alterations.
- AutoDelete function eliminates Dynamic connectors linking one shape to another when the linked shapes are deleted. Visio will also delete a dynamic connector and reattach the second to both remaining shapes if you remove a shape between two others.

To employ AutoAdd, simply drag a shape onto an existing dynamic connector. When you position the new shape over a dynamic connector before releasing it, Visio activates AutoAdd, signified by solid green squares added to the connector's ends.

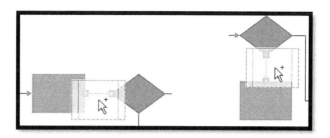

Here's a sample diagram that we'll adjust using Auto-add and Auto-delete. Pay attention to the positions of the unconnected shapes in the upper right.

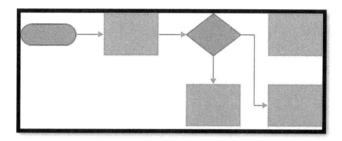

Here's what happens when you drop a subprocess shape onto the connector below the decision diamond.

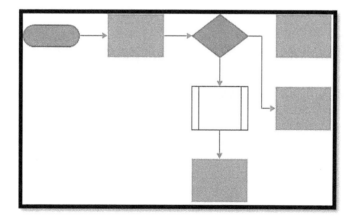

Utilize AutoAdd

- Connect two shapes together using a dynamic connector.

Drag a stenciled shape onto the dynamic connector.

Employ Auto-delete

To utilize AutoDelete, simply delete the connected shape. For instance, if you remove the bottom process shape in the figure above, Visio will automatically delete the dynamic connector between the shapes.

Utilizing AutoDelete

When you delete a shape connected to two other shapes, Visio will combine the remaining connectors into one.

Summary

This chapter guides you through the process of utilizing the Dynamic Grid to align, position, and resize shapes. Additionally, it covers selecting, copying, pasting, and duplicating shapes, placing them with rulers and guides, resizing, repositioning, and rotating them, connecting shapes with lines and dynamic connectors, employing AutoConnect and Quick Shapes, as well as utilizing AutoAdd and AutoDelete functionalities.

Chapter 3

Manage Text, Shapes and Pages

In the initial two chapters, you explored the Visio user interface and discovered various methods to incorporate shapes into a design. For many diagrams, the subsequent logical progression is to integrate text into the shapes. Subsequently, you might find it necessary to adjust the position, rotation, or formatting of the text to suit specific shapes. Additionally, numerous diagrams call for text-only shapes, comments, or screen tips.

Unlike previous program versions, Visio now facilitates the easy replacement of one shape with another. However, there are situations where it's beneficial or necessary to change multiple shapes simultaneously. Additionally, there might be instances where an alternative shape is preferred over the one currently on the page. This chapter will address all of these scenarios.

Lastly, distributing information or visuals across multiple pages often proves advantageous. Instead of repeatedly copying and pasting the same text boxes and shapes onto each page, you can create background pages to contain the recurring content and then assign those background pages to the foreground pages to achieve the desired outcome.

In this chapter, you'll be guided through the steps required to handle shape text, create and format text boxes, add ScreenTips and comments to shapes, insert images, replace and group shapes, understand and utilize layers, and manage pages.

Manage the Shape Text

While many Visio shapes are functional on their own, there are occasions when including text within a shape is necessary to complete a diagram. In Visio, you have the option to either create a text-only shape or add text to an existing shape, integrating it as part of the shape. You'll explore the first method in this topic and the second method in the section of this chapter titled "Create and format text boxes."

Add Text to Shapes

Most shapes are designed to accommodate text in one of the three methods outlined in the instructions following this section. While the text might initially appear anywhere, when added to objects like form objects, it typically appears in the center. (You'll learn how to reposition the text on a form in the following section.) Variations in text placement can occur due to decisions made by shape designers or actions taken by Visio users.

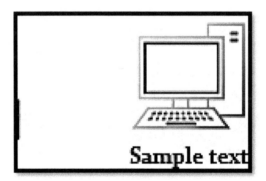

As shape designers determine the placement of text on a shape and may restrict text entry or modifications, you may encounter such shapes while browsing Visio diagrams. Unfortunately, it's not visually apparent whether a shape's text has been locked. For example, in this image, the square on the right shows

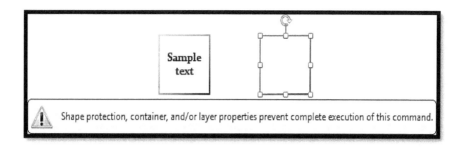

To add text to shapes, begin with one of the following options:

- o Choose a shape, then enter text directly into it.
- o Double-click on a shape, then type text within it.
- o Enter edit mode by pressing F2, click on a shape, and then type text.

Exiting Text Entry Mode

Begin with one of the following options:

- o Click anywhere outside the shape to exit.
- o Press the Esc key.
- o Press F2.

Activate Text Entry Termination Using the Enter key by Following these steps:

- o Display the Backstage View.
- o Click on Options to access the Visio Options dialog box.

In the Visio Options dialog box, select Advanced, then check the box labeled "Press ENTER to commit shape text." This setting requires pressing Shift+Enter to input multiline text within a shape.

Adjust the Position and Size of Shape Text

A text block is an independent object that contains the text within a Visio shape. You can move and modify the text block separately from its parent shape using Visio's Text Box tool. Additionally, there are various buttons available on the Home tab that allow you to adjust the position of text within a text block.

This image clearly illustrates the concept of the text block's independence. If you use the Pointer Tool to click on the city shape, as depicted on the left, a selection rectangle will appear around the city icon. However, if you use the Text Block tool to click on the city shape, as shown on the right, you'll see the selection rectangle along with all the usual control knobs.

In Visio, you have the flexibility to adjust the size of the text block by moving its resizable handle. Additionally, you can relocate the entire text block to a different location.

Nearly every aspect of the text shape can be modified using the buttons within the Font and Paragraph categories on the Home tab. Of particular relevance to this section are the six text alignment buttons within the Paragraph group, which enable you to control the position of the text within a text block.

To Activate the Text Block Function

Select the Text Block tool from the Tools group on the Home tab.

To Move a Shape's Text Block

- Begin by selecting the shape using the Text Block tool to move the text block to a new location.

To Resize the Text Block on a Shape

- With the Text Block tool selected, first, choose the shape, and then adjust any resized handles.

To Adjust the Text Alignment Within the Text Block

- Choose one of the text alignment buttons in the Paragraph group under the Home tab.

Or

- To begin, right-click a shape.
- After clicking the Align Text button on the mini toolbar, select any of the nine alignment buttons.

Adjust the Orientation of Shape Text

The orientation of text in a Visio shape may either match the orientation of the shape itself or be quite different. (It's worth noting that Visio add-in code could potentially alter text orientation, although this aspect is not addressed in the following examples.) The discrepancy is typically attributed to the design of the shape and the formulas integrated within it.

Please be aware that the text within a shape usually rotates along with the shape itself. This behavior is default for text in a Visio shape.

When selecting multiple shapes and rotating the entire selection, the behavior of text on the selected shapes may not be consistent. In the image provided, the first set of shapes displays upright text on the selected shapes, with one shape featuring an arrow-like dynamic connector pointing to the right. In the other two sets, the connector text remains upright, while the text inside the circle and square are rotated to align with the respective shapes. This illustrates how a shape utilizes formulas to modify the behavior of shape text.

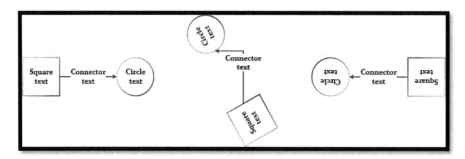

Several other text behaviors exist. In the image below, you can observe the right arrow shape from the raised blocks stencil in the block diagram template. The text does not conform to the orientation of the shapes, nor is it aligned straight. Instead, a formula within the shape maintains the text at multiples of 45 degrees.

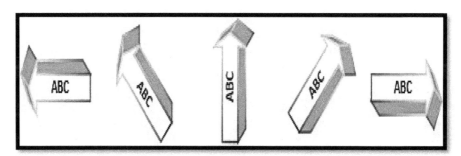

With the Visio user interface, you have the ability to change the orientation of text within a shape and adjust the text angle using embedded formulas. The illustration shows the 2-D Single arrows from the Block stencils in the Basic Shapes template. By default, unless you exert full control through the Text Block tool introduced in the previous section, the text on the arrow rotates along with the arrow itself. The effects of solely rotating the text block are demonstrated in this image.

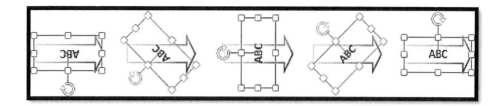

To Rotate a Shape

Select from the options below:

- After choosing the shape, drag the rotation handle.
- After selecting the shape, open the Size & Position window, and modify the Angle value.
- Click the Position button in the Rotate Shapes group of the Arrange group on the Home tab, then choose one of the options from the Rotate or Flip menu.

To Alternate between Several Shapes

Select two or more shapes, then make your selection from the following options:

- Rotate the Rotation handle in a circle.
- After pointing to Rotate Shapes, select an option from the Rotate or Flip menu by clicking the Position button.

Merely Rotating the Words—not the shape

- Choose the Text Block 2 from the Tools section of the Home tab.
- Drag the handle to rotate the shape that contains the text.

Creating and Arranging the Text Fields

Using the Text tool, you can create text-only shapes as well as add text to existing shapes. When a text box is initially added to the page, it inherits the default font, paragraph formatting, and other settings, as illustrated on the left side of the image below.

In our illustration, the same text box can be seen on the right with a significantly different appearance. However, once the text box is added, it becomes another Visio shape on the page. Consequently, you can modify its text properties as well as apply themes, variations, effects, or other shape formatting elements.

Visio users often encounter a common mistake when they need to add a label to a shape: they create a separate text box, input text within it, and then position the text box on top of or adjacent to the object.

This approach places the text near the shape but does not integrate the text as part of the shape. This has two main drawbacks: firstly, moving the shape does not automatically relocate the text, and secondly, it prevents running a report that consolidates the text associated with each shape. The significance of the latter might not be immediately apparent, but it will become more evident in later chapters.

Here's how to generate a Text box:

- o Navigate to the Home tab within the Tools group and click on the Text button.
- o Alternatively, you can press **Ctrl+2**.
- o Right-click and select the Drawing Tools button, then choose either Horizontal Text Box or Vertical Text Box from the drop-down menu.
- o Drag to add a text box.

Incorporate ScreenTips and Comments

To provide additional ad hoc information to readers, you can include ScreenTips and comments in your diagrams.

Although they serve similar functions, they possess highly varied characteristics.

- **ScreenTips**: While they remain invisible otherwise, they display pop-up text when you hover over shapes. A ScreenTip remains unseen until you hover over a shape with one, at which point it becomes visible.
- **Comments**: Comments are distinguished by a unique icon indicating their presence, but you need to click on the icon to access the comment text. Each comment displays the author's name and creation date alongside. Since Visio 2013, a single comment shape can include threaded comments from multiple authors, with each entry shown in the order it was submitted.

If you add a comment to a single shape, it will be associated specifically with that shape. However, if you select two or more shapes before adding a comment, the comment will be linked to the anchor shape. Subsequent chapters will cover "Adding style, color, and themes," which provides further insight into anchor shapes.

Prior to 2013, comments in Visio were only tied to a page, not to individual shapes. Therefore, when you add a comment without selecting any shapes, it is added to the drawing page. In earlier versions of Visio, if you move a shape with an associated comment, the shape will move correctly, but the comment will not.

Consider the following factors when deciding whether to use ScreenTips or comments:

- Employ ScreenTips for conveying helpful yet non-essential information about a shape, but keep in mind that viewers might not be aware of the presence of a ScreenTip.
- Opt for comments when you wish to notify readers of a comment's existence, when you want multiple individuals to engage in a threaded discussion, and when it's beneficial to identify the authorship and timing of comments.

Here are some examples of ScreenTips and comments. As the pointer hovers over the chair shape, the ScreenTip is displayed above the chair. Additionally, the word "Comments" appears as the pointer approaches the comment indicator, which is shown in a comment balloon just above the top right corner of the sofa shape.

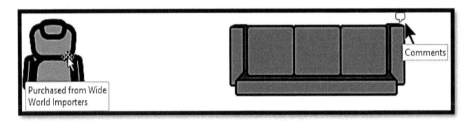

Choose a comment indicator displaying the text of the most recent comments. In the image provided, comments from various authors are visible. If a shape has multiple comments, each one can be collapsed individually.

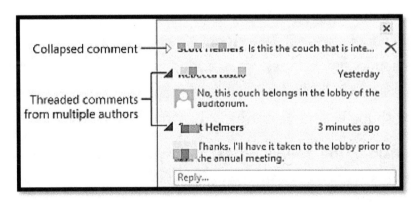

Visio provides a Comments window, visible in the image, where you can view all comments in a document collectively. Clicking on a shape in the commenting pane highlights the shape containing the comment. If you click on a comment for a shape on the current page, Visio will bring the shape into view (if it isn't already visible) and highlight the comment indicator in blue.

If you click on a comment for a shape that is located on a different page, Visio will navigate to that page.

Here's how to include ScreenTips:

- o Select a shape, then click on the ScreenTip button located in the Text group of the Insert tab to reveal a dialog box for Shape ScreenTip.

o Input your desired text into the Shape ScreenTip popup, then click **OK** to confirm.

How to Open or Close the Comments panel

Press the top section of the Comments Panel button found in the Remarks group on the Review tab.

To add notes to a shape

o Once you've selected a shape, click on the "**New Comment**" button located beside the Remarks group on the Review tab.

Tap on the "Create Comment" button after choosing a shape in the Remarks pane.

Or

After right-clicking on a shape, select "**Add Comment**".

o Input your comment, then click anywhere else on the page.

Commenting on a Page

Tap the New Comment button beneath the Comments group on the Review tab, but make sure nothing is chosen first.
Or

Once you have right-clicked on a page space, select Add Comment from the context menu. Once text has been added, select outside the comment box.

To Comment in Response

In case the Comment window is closed, hit the remark icon on a shape or page and subsequently select Respond.
Or

Locate the appropriate comment, click Respond, if the Comment window is open. Also, you have the option to choose a location outside of the comment area and type your response. To display or conceal the comment indicator, navigate to the comments group on the review tab, click the comments pane arrow, and then choose reveal tags.

Insert pictures

In preceding sections, we explored the creation of text boxes and shapes by dragging masters from a stencil. However, there are instances where utilizing a picture to construct a shape is preferable. Thankfully, Visio simplifies this process. You can easily search for images from various web sources and import photos or images in any popular file format from your computer. The available sources on the author's PC are displayed here.

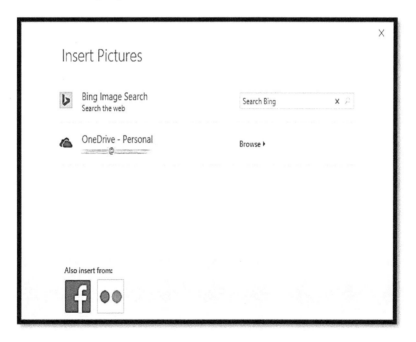

Presented here are a photograph, a clip art icon, and an online flag image.

Here's how to include an image from a network drive or your computer

- o Select the "**Image**" button located in the Illustrations category on the Insert tab.
- o Browse to the desired location, choose the image file, and click "Open."

To Add an Image Sourced from the Internet

- o Select the "**Online Images**" button within the Illustrations category on the Insert tab.
- o Enter your search terms into the Bing Image Search text box.

Or

Select OneDrive or another image source by clicking on it.

- o After choosing the desired image, click "**Insert**."

Replace Shapes

Ever since Visio was first created, users have yearned for the ability to replace a shape on the drawing page with an entirely new one while maintaining all of the previous shape's important features. That feature was finally made available in Visio 2013, and in Visio 2016, it is an important consideration.

Understanding the capabilities of the replace shape feature can be easily gained by looking at the Figure. To build the diagram in the picture, the Directional Map template (not the Directional Map 3D template) from the Maps and Floor Plans template category was utilized.

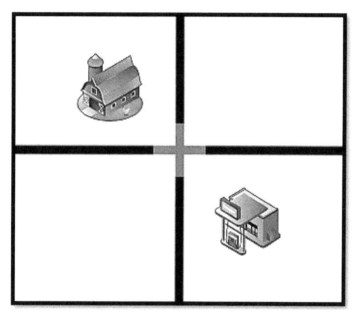

Even though it is much more important than the previous intersection, the cloverleaf still follows all four road segments and maintains the color and shape of the previous intersection; you can perform a straightforward swap, such as transforming the barn into a stadium, or a more complex one, such as transforming the four-way intersection into a full-sized highway cloverleaf, via the replace shape option (both illustrated in this figure). Both modifications only needed a single click from the user, but the new intersection necessitated more intricate changes in the background.

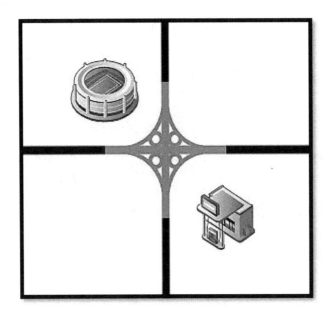

However, if you select "**Change Shape**," the active stencils will display available shapes. Alternatively, you can choose a shape from a menu. If the desired shape isn't already selected in one of the open stencils, open the desired stencil before selecting the "**Change Shape**" option. This allows you to choose from tens of thousands of alternative shapes to substitute for one shape in a drawing.

After selecting one or more shapes, choose the "**Change Shape**" option located in the Editing group on the Home tab.

Or

- Right-click on a shape, then choose "**Change Shape**" from the small toolbar that appears.
- Select the replacement shape of your choice.

Next, utilize a master from a different stencil to substitute shapes.

- Click on the "**More Shapes**" button located within the Shapes window. If the stencil you want isn't already open, click on its title to open it.

90

o Opt for the "**Shape Change**" option.

o Position your cursor over the downward arrow adjacent to the current stencil's name.

o Click on the name of the specific shape within the stencil to access its gallery.

o Select the replacement shape that best fits your needs.

Group Shapes

Up until now, your focus has primarily been on handling simple, clearly defined shapes.

In Visio, grouped sets of shapes are quite common, driven by various factors, as outlined below:

- Managing or manipulating a group of shapes is simpler compared to dealing with multiple individual objects.

Image shape designers often aim for a more sophisticated appearance or behavior due to several reasons, including:

Add text to the form at different positions:

- Display different colors on different shapes within a group.
- Enable various components of the shape to respond differently to environmental changes.
- Ensure alignment of the subgroup's components.

This example showcases four forms extracted from the Department stencils within the Work Flow Diagram design, assembled on the drawing page, illustrating the initial scenario. On the left side of the diagram, the four distinct shapes are displayed. A single click changes the fill color of each of the four shapes in the center. Subsequently, a second click alters the color, and the group's handle is adjusted to resize all four shapes on the right side. Performing actions such as moving, copying, and pasting on the group shape allows you to manipulate all four shapes collectively.

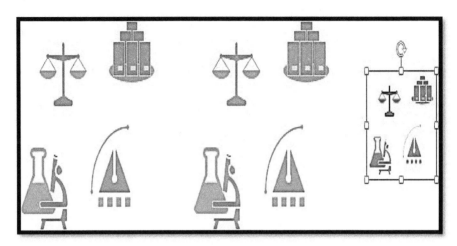

A group functions as a shape, akin to the individual shapes comprising it. Utilizing a group shape, you can perform various actions on any included shape, such as applying borders or fills, inserting text and columns, and incorporating shape data. Selecting a shape within a group requires two clicks; Visio defaults to selecting the group with the first click.

This image showcases the utilization of groups to create intricate shapes; several departmental shapes have been grouped together. These forms were crafted by combining various elements or images. Another instance of complex shape design is depicted in the image. Shapes on the right originate from the Compliance Shapes stencil, while those on the left are derived from the Furniture stencil, which is part of the Maps and Floor Plans template group within the Business template group. Many of the masters in Visio stencils consist of groups of shapes, much like these seven shapes.

Exercise caution when contemplating ungrouping a shape that you didn't create. Why? Because many grouped shapes inherit characteristics from the group's sub-shapes. For example, attributes like size, color, or position of a sub-shape can be influenced by values within the group. Unnecessarily ungrouping a shape results in the loss of all its properties—its shape geometry, shape data, and everything else.

To Merge Multiple Shapes

- Click the Group button, then select Group under the Arrange group on the Home tab.
- Right-click any of the selected shapes and choose Group from the context menu.
- Press Ctrl+ G.
- Click "Ctrl+Shift+ G."

To Ungroup a Set of Shapes

- Tap the Group button in the Arrange group on the Home tab, then select Ungroup.
- To group or ungroup any of the selected shapes, use the right-click menu.
- Press Ctrl+Shift+U.

Selecting a shape from a group

- o To select the group, tap on the group shape.
- o Then, select the desired shape.

Managing Layers

Visio shapes can be organized into layers to control and manage their different attributes. Unlike in some drawing programs, Visio layers are not positioned "**in front of**" or "**behind**" other layers. Instead, shapes are assigned to layers to provide control over features such as whether layer components are printable, displayed on the drawing page, or selectable.

For example, in a floor plan design, furniture could be assigned to one layer, walls and structural elements to another, and electrical wiring to a third.

Subsequently, you can utilize layer properties to perform the following tasks:

- o Lock the layers containing the wiring and infrastructure when rearranging furniture.
- o Hide the layer containing the furniture to view the entire available space.
- o Keep the electrical wiring visible on the screen, but adjust the layer's settings to prevent the printing of the wiring.
- o Select all shapes on the selected layer or layers.

Layers provide significant flexibility in managing complex drawing elements, making them indispensable. Given their potential complexity, it's advisable to plan your layer system ahead of time: a shape may reside on one, multiple, or none of the layers within a drawing page. Each layer possesses seven attributes.

Below are the seven attributes of a layer:

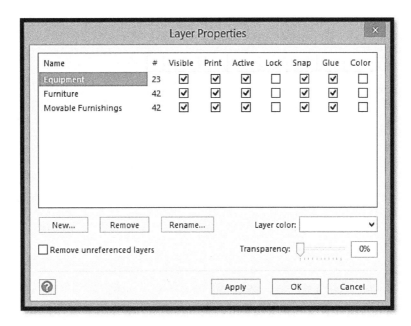

In numerous Visio templates, shapes from corresponding stencils are automatically assigned to predefined layers. The layers seen in this image were incorporated into the diagram by dragging shapes from the Furniture stencil within the Maps And Floor Plans group. Similar to these, templates like Flowchart and Engineering also feature predefined layers.

The Layer Properties control box comprises seven properties, listed as follows:

- **Visible**: Manages the visibility of shapes on a layer within the drawing page.
- **Print:** Include or exclude a layer's contents from printing.
- **Active**: Ensures that the layer is updated with any new shapes added to the page. When multiple layers are active simultaneously, new shapes are added to each of the active layers.

- **Lock**: When Image Lock is activated, you are unable to select, move, or alter any shapes on the layer. Additionally, a locked layer prohibits the addition of further shapes.
- **Snap and glue:** Specify whether snapping or gluing other shapes to the shapes on this layer is permitted.
- **Color Clearing**: This option reverts the colors of layer members to their default settings. Image Color temporarily alters the colors of all objects on a layer. The Layer Color and Transparency options in the lower right of the dialog box become active when you select the Color attribute for a layer.

Groups and layers serve to organize sets of shapes, yet it's important to understand their distinct purposes and behaviors. For instance, when a group is selected and moved or resized, its constituent shapes are collectively affected. Conversely, when you select and move or resize a shape on a layer, only that particular shape is impacted; other shapes remain unaffected. Additionally, layers offer capabilities such as locking, hiding, and other operations on all shapes within the layer, which are not possible with groups.

It's essential to recognize that groups and layers are not mutually exclusive; there are often valid reasons for utilizing both within the same diagram.

Adding a Layer to a Page

- After selecting the Layers button under the Editing group on the Home tab, click on Layer Properties.
- Within the Layer Properties window, click on the New button.
- In the Create Layer dialog box, enter a name for the layer, then click OK twice.

You may also:

- o   Select a shape.

- o   Choose Assign to Layer under the Layers button within the Editing group on the Home tab.

- o   Click on the **New button** in the Layer dialog box.

- o   Enter a layer name into the Create Layer dialog box, then click OK twice.

Copy and paste a shape linked to a layer from one page to another. If a layer with the same name already exists on the destination page, the duplicated shape will be added to it.

Or

Drag a shape onto the drawing page from one of the stencils within the Basic Flowchart design or another template featuring pre-built layers.

You Can Delete a Layer from a Page

- o   After selecting the Layers button under the Editing group on the Home tab, click on Layer Properties.
- o   Within the Layer Properties dialog box, select the name of the layer you want to delete.
- o   Tap the Erase button, then respond to the alert accordingly.

To close the Layer Properties dialog box, select **OK**

Modify Layer Properties

To modify the properties of a layer, open the Layer Properties dialog box, select or remove the desired properties, and then hit **OK**.

Adding a shape to a layer

- The Editing group on the Home tab has a Layers option. Click Assign to Layer.
- To assign the shape to the layer or layers that you have selected in the Layers dialog box, hit **OK**.

The following procedures can also be followed:

- Select a stencil from the Basic Flowchart template or any other template with integrated layers and drag it onto the drawing page.

You can remove a shape from a layer

- In the Editing group of the Home tab, choose Assign to Layer from the Layers button.
- Select the layer or layers in the Layer dialog box that you wish to remove the shape from, and then hit **OK**.

To select every shape on a layer

- On the Home tab, in the Editing group, tap the Select button and then Select by Type.
- In the select by type tab, choose the layer, check the layer you want, and hit **OK**.

Manage Shapes

A Visio drawing's pages can individually have different dimensions, measurement units, and other properties since they are independent from one another. This allows for the blending of landscape and portrait pages as well as various page sizes into a single diagram.

Within each page, Visio maintains distinct settings for the drawing page that is displayed on screen and the page that is printed.

This differentiation can serve purposes such as the following:

- Shrink a drawing to fit onto a smaller piece of paper.
- Print a drawing on a large piece of paper.
- Print a drawing across multiple sheets of paper.

Visio pages can be broadly categorized into two groups:

Foreground: These pages, frequently printed or distributed through various means, encompass the actual drawing content.

Background Pages: These encompass page elements and shapes that can be configured to appear on one or multiple pages. However, items on background pages cannot be selected or altered unless the backdrop page is active.

Given that you may need to link to background pages from other pages, they prove to be quite beneficial. Once linked, all text and visuals from the background pages are replicated on the connected pages.

In a common scenario, elements such as a border, page number, page name, and possibly a watermark or other design feature are positioned on a background page to consistently appear in the same location on every foreground page.

Another common application involves incorporating the corporate logo, a legal disclaimer, and any other desired graphics or text intended to appear across multiple pages onto a background page. Keep in mind that a diagram can feature multiple background pages, particularly when it spans several pages. Consequently, specific foreground pages may showcase content from a designated background page, while others may utilize different background pages, resulting in varied designs.

The most common scenario involves linking a foreground page to a background page. However, you can also establish connections between background pages, creating a hierarchical structure of page content that can be creatively and efficiently shared across multiple foreground pages.

Utilizing the Foreground Pages

Managing foreground pages requires the use of the two page name buttons located at the bottom of the drawing window. By right-clicking an existing page name tab, you can carry out any action from the shortcut menu.

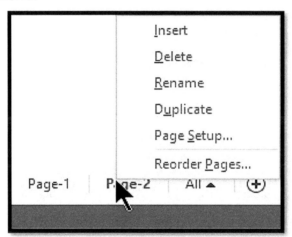

When you incorporate a foreground page into the diagram, Visio configures the attributes for the new page based on the properties of the current active page. For example, if Page-3 is linked to a background page and has a landscape orientation with metric measurements, these properties will be inherited by your new page and the connection to the background page.

Incorporating a new page into your diagram is straightforward if all existing pages are configured similarly. Before clicking "**Insert**," it's advisable to select the current page that closely resembles the one you intend to add, especially if your diagram features foreground pages with varying orientations, measurement units, background pages, or printer paper settings.

Visio has the capability to replicate not only a page's attributes but also its contents. This feature, introduced with Visio 2013, fulfills a longstanding request from Visio users.

To promptly link the current foreground page with a new foreground page

- Right-click on the page name tab, then click "**Insert**."
- If not already selected, choose "**Foreground**" in the Page Setup tab of the Page Setup dialog box.
- Optionally, modify the page's name.
- Click "**OK**."

Incorporate a new foreground page into the current one

- Opt for "Insert Page (**+**)" from the menu.
- Choose the "**New Page**" option under the Pages category on the Insert tab (not its arrow).
- Click on the arrow next to "Blank Page" under the Pages category on the Insert tab.

Changing the name of a page

- Double-click on the tab for the page name you want to change, then type the new name.
- Press Enter.

Or

- Click anywhere except the page name tab.
- To rearrange pages, drag the page name tab to the left or right.

As the destination tab location for your page is displayed at the bottom of the drawing window, dragging tabs with the page name offers an easy method to reorder pages. However, the following approach might be simpler if your diagram contains numerous pages and the destination tab is concealed.

- Rearrange Pages by right-clicking a page name tab.
- In the Reorder Pages dialog box, depicted in the Figure, select the page name you want to move, then use the Move Up or Move Down button to position the page as needed.

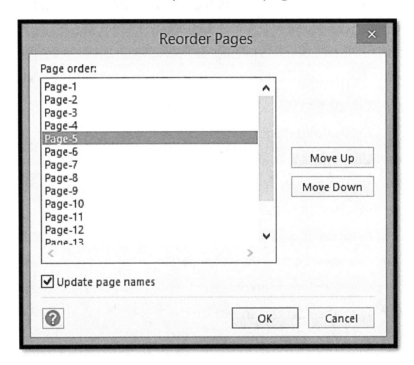

- Tap the **OK** button.

To Delete a Page

Right-click on a page title tab and choose the option "**Delete**."

Creating a Duplicate of a page

Choose any one of the following options:

- Right-click on the page title tab and choose "**Duplicate**."

- Within the Pages group, click the New Page arrows on the Insert tab, then choose "**Duplicate This Page**."

Set up the Foreground pages

Arrange foreground pages In the Page Setup dialog box, most page setup functions are accessible via one of the five tabs. The Page Properties box is shown in the image below as you enter the Page Setup dialog box.

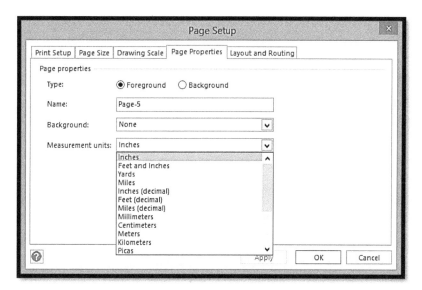

On the Page Setup tab, users can modify the page category, assign a new page name, select a background page, and customize the page's measurement units. Take note of the navigation bar in the Measuring Units menu—there are up to 20 options available. The effects of changing the measuring units are immediately visible in the rulers at the top and bottom of the drawing page. Additionally, the options available on the Print Setup tab serve as the primary method to adjust the size and layout of the physical page for printing purposes.

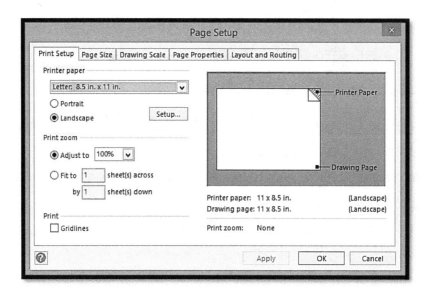

You can adjust the following settings on the Print Setup tab:

- **Printers paper**: Select a paper size for the printer. As depicted in the Figure, most US Unit designs typically default to letter-sized paper, while A4 is the most common metric template size. Additionally, various other preset paper sizes are available regardless of the default. You can also choose between Portrait and Landscape orientations.

- **Print Zoom**: If your drawing appears larger or smaller than usual, you may adjust the default zoom level of Adapt To 100% included in many layouts. Utilize a zoom level greater than 100% to spread your drawing across multiple sheets of paper.

- **Fit to**: For an alternative method, utilize this one to scale your design for printing.

- **Print**: The only setting in this section alters whether gridlines appear in printed results or not. Gridlines are normally not included in templates.

o When you edit your print settings, the preview pane on the right side of the page updates dynamically to show your current print settings both textually and graphically.

The Page Size tab allows you to modify the drawing page's parameters, as seen in the image; changes made here do not apply instantly to the printed page.

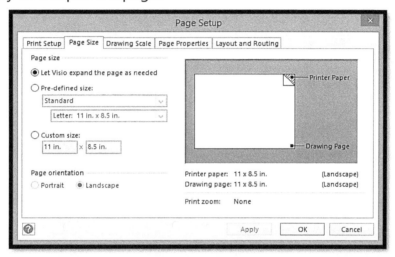

Along with a preview pane, the Page Size tab contains two configurable sectors:

Page size: The first application in this part permits a dynamic Auto Size feature. The following options can also be used to establish a page size using a preset list or by giving exact instructions.

Page orientation: The options in the Page Size section become active if you choose Pre-Defined Dimension or Custom Dimension. These options allow you to change the alignment of the drawing page to the actual page.

To Adjust Printer Paper Settings

▪ To access Page Setup, right-click on a tab-titled page and choose it from the menu that displays.

- From the Page Setup dialog box, select the Print Setup tab.
- After making the necessary changes, click OK.

To Change the orientation of the page

- Open the Page Setup dialog box, go to the Print Setup tab, choose either Portrait or Landscape, and tap OK.

To Modify the size of the drawing page

- In the Page Setup category, click the Size button, then choose the preferred page size.

Or

- The Page Setting dialog box will appear. Choose the Page Size tab.
- Hit OK after choosing a pre-defined size and one of the standard paper sizes.

After choosing Custom size, type in the desired page width and height in the corresponding fields, and then hit **OK**.

Control Auto Size

Auto Size is a page configuration setting that can be either helpful or inconvenient. Its purpose is to automatically expand the drawing page whenever you drag a shape beyond the current page boundaries. The shape retains its previous position, and the pointer shows its new location. In this example, a circle is being moved off the page to the right. Visio responds by adding a new page, indicated by the white page-sized rectangle on the gray canvas.

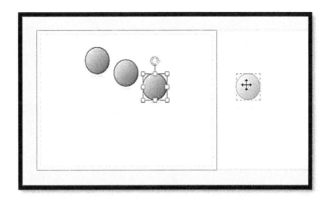

Visio can shrink the expanded page if you delete or move the last shape from an extended section of the drawing page. The Auto Size function works both vertically and horizontally, so if users add or move shapes above or below the current page, Visio will add the necessary pages accordingly. When Auto Size is turned off, Visio does not expand the drawing page. Auto Size is enabled in certain templates but disabled in others. However, you can adjust the Auto Size setting as needed.

The Auto Size feature is enabled on a per-page basis. Therefore, changing the settings for the present page does not impact other pages.

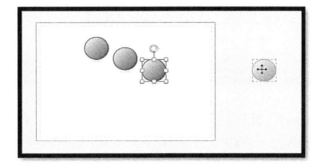

To Activate or Deactivate Auto Size

- Choose the Auto Size option located within the Page Settings group on the Design tab.

Or

- On a tab with the name "page," right-click and choose "Page Setup" from the menu that displays.
- Select the Page Setting dialog box's Page Size tab.
- After choosing Allow Visio to Expand the Page as Necessary or one of the Other Page Size Options, hit OK.

Experiment with Borders and Background pages

Several features discussed in this section will automatically generate background pages for you. You can also create background pages manually. In either case, background pages are used to consolidate graphics and text that need to appear on multiple pages.

Apply Background and Borders Automatically

The core of automatic background page creation lies in two buttons within the Background and variations group on the Design tab, illustrated here.

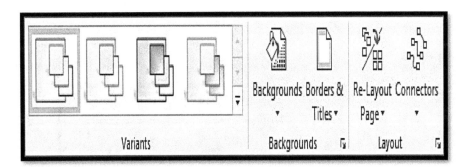

Backgrounds: This button presents a gallery of images suitable for use as website background images.

Borders and titles: This button shows a gallery of border designs with a title text block; many also include a page number, and some feature a date.

Clicking a button in either gallery enables Visio to do three things:
- Create a background page called VBackground-1.
- Add the background page's desired border, title, or image.
- The currently active foreground page is connected to from the backdrop page.

This image illustrates the result of adding the Flow background image to a foreground page with three square shapes.

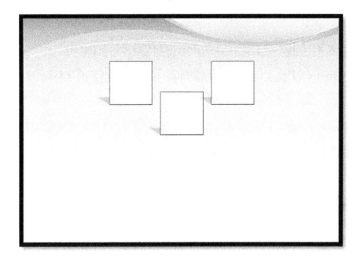

To apply and create a background page instantly

Take one of the following actions:
- On the Design tab, within the Backgrounds group, click the Backgrounds button, then choose one of the gallery's background images.
- In the Backgrounds group on the Design tab, click the Borders & Titles button, then select any of the border/title combinations from the gallery.

1. Choose Page Setup from the menu that displays when you right-click on the page name tab.
2. Hit OK after selecting None from the Background list in the Page Setup section of the Page Setup dialog box.

Manually Applying Background Pages

You can manually add a background page just as you would add foreground pages; however, you must ensure that the page type is set to background at the appropriate time. When you create a manual background page, Visio assigns it a name in the format Background-1.

After creating a background page, you can link it to one or more existing pages. However, it is essential to take note that you can only link a background page to one page at a time.

All page properties, including the assignment of the background page, are duplicated whenever you insert a new page. Choose one page to use as your backdrop page and make that your active page when adding other pages if you want to utilize the same background page for multiple new pages.

Creating a Background Page Manually

- Choose the Page Setup tab in the Page Setup dialogue box by right-clicking the page name tab, choosing Insert, and then choosing Background.

Or

- Hit Background Page after selecting the New Page icon (not its button) on the Insert tab within the Pages group.
- Change the background page's title if you want to.
- Hit the OK button.

Assigning a Background Page Manually

- Navigate to the foreground page where the background is to be established, and then select the Page Setup tab in the Page Setup dialog box.
- After choosing a page from the Background list, hit **OK**.

Select none from the backdrop list on the page configuration tab of the dialog box that appears, then click **OK** to remove the manually defined background page of a foreground page.

Summary

In this chapter, we covered various aspects of working with shapes, including managing them, creating and formatting text boxes, using screen tips and comments, and inserting pictures. After reading this chapter, you should have a better understanding of how to work with a Visio diagram, especially when it involves shapes.

Chapter 4

Design a Business Procedure Diagram

Building a business process diagram with a flowchart template makes sense, since Microsoft states that about one-third of Visio diagrams are created using templates from the Flowchart category.

Flowcharts, swimlane diagrams, and Business Process Model and Notation (BPMN) diagrams are the three types of business process diagrams that you will create in this chapter using the most popular templates.

If your goal is to sketch the logic of a software module rather than document business operations, the diagram creation methods described below will still be helpful. In this chapter, we will guide you through selecting a flowchart template, creating a flowchart, and understanding swimlane diagrams, among other topics.

Select a Flow Chart Template

The standard edition includes a few basic flowchart templates, while the professional edition offers a larger selection.

Visio Standard

The Work Flow Diagram and Work Flow Diagram - 3D templates are also part of the Flowchart category, as shown in the image. The former, introduced in Visio 2013, is a theme-compatible diagram format for mapping workflows and includes stencils with updated, modern designs. If you prefer the earlier style of workflow diagrams from previous versions of Visio, the latter template is available.

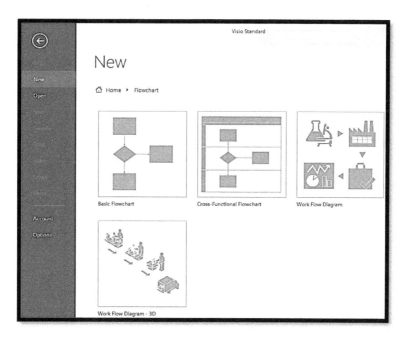

Visio Professional

You get the five additional templates in addition to the four in the standard edition in the professional edition. SDL, IDEF0, BPMN and two Microsoft SharePoint workflows—one for SharePoint 2010 and the other for SharePoint 2016—are all supported.

Sidebar: Vertical or Horizontal?

Artists have debated whether flowcharts should be drawn horizontally (landscape) or vertically (portrait) for years. Supporters who lean vertically favor a top-to-bottom arrangement, while those who lean horizontally favor a left-to-right (or right-to-left) one.

You may create any type of flowchart in Visio, however the default layout is landscape—possibly because most modern monitors are widescreen. The flowchart's default orientation was portrait prior to Visio 2010.

Create Flow Charts

This subject explores how to use the Basic Flowchart template to create a diagram. You may create flowcharts like the recruiting one for human resources using the skills and information in the following piece.

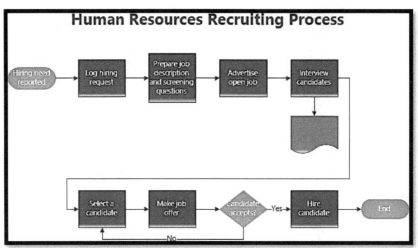

You will notice right away while working with flowcharts that they are perfect candidates to take advantage of the AutoConnect and Quick Shapes features that are covered in Chapter 2, "Build diagrams." These characteristics work particularly well with flowcharts, but they are useful with other types of diagrams as well.

A start/end form is where a flowchart starts. Every process box denotes a distinct phase within the comprehensive process. Process shapes can be quickly added using the Quick Shapes option.

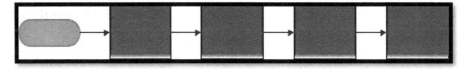

Here, you'll see how simple it is to use the Dynamic Grid to relocate the first page within the second row of the flow chart so that the new shape aligns with the pre-existing process shape.

114

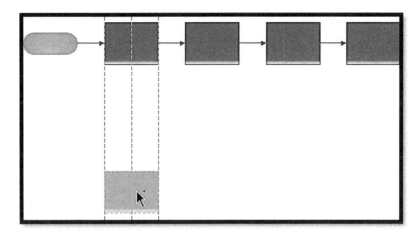

With the Quick Shapes tiny toolbar, you can place shapes directly onto the page, making finishing the second row as easy as finishing the first, as seen in the image. The process flow is completed by the decision diamond and second start/end form in the second row.

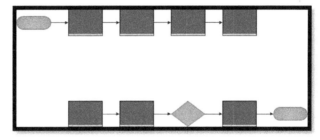

Here is an interesting substitute for the document shape insert. The primary shape selected in the stencil is copied by Visio and placed on the page whenever you click the AutoConnect arrow beneath a shape.

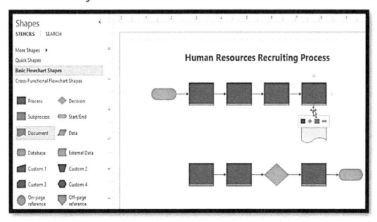

Just before you click the AutoConnect arrow, Visio shows you a semitransparent preview of the form that will be added to the diagram.

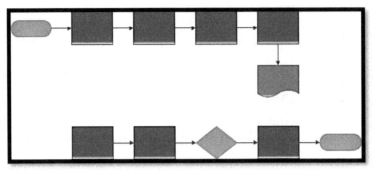

The Stages to Finish a Flow Chart are as Follows:

- If there are many rows in the flowchart, link the final shape in the top row to the first shape in the bottom row.
- There should always be a second path to follow for each decision diamond you include. (You may include more than two possible outcomes if there are any.)
- Each shape has to have the text added to it.

For reasons that are detailed in the "Dynamic or static glue?" sidebar on the following page, the dynamic connector that runs from top right to bottom left was attached to both shapes inside the completed flowchart that is shown here using static glue. You may build the second decision outcome at the bottom of the page using either static or dynamic glue.

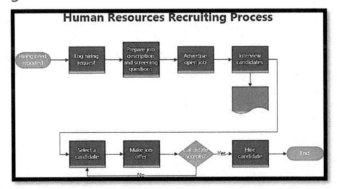

To Quickly Generate a Flowchart

- A Start/End shape should be placed on the page.
- Use the AutoConnect arrows to add additional shapes to the same row.
- Use the Dynamic Grid to position a shape beneath a form in the upper row after dragging it into the page to begin the lower row.
- Expand the second row's shape selection by using the AutoConnect arrow.

Sidebar: Dynamic or Static glue

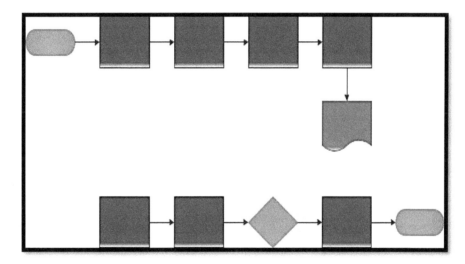

The placement of the two forms on the page may affect your decision between static and dynamic glue when you need to unite them with a connector. By connecting the process boxes at the top right and bottom left of this image, for instance, one method of creating dynamic glue can be applied. Overlapping connectors should be avoided if a suitable replacement is available, even though the output is a perfectly valid flowchart.

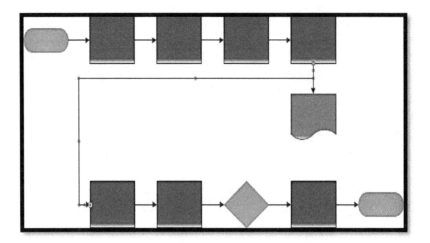

Applying static glue from the point of connection on the upper-right shape's right side to the lower-left shape's left point of connection yields a more acceptable result.

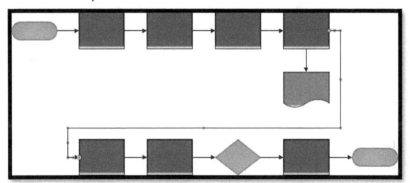

The second decision outcome has been added to the bottom of the diagram and can be achieved using either static or dynamic glue.

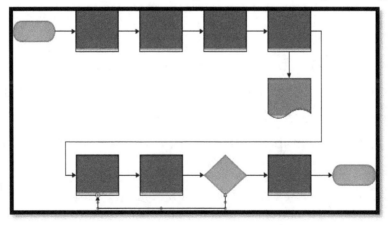

Select any combination from the list below:

- Use the dragging method to select a form from the Basic Flowchart Shapes stencil.
- To move the selected master from the Basic Flowchart Shapes stencils onto the page, utilize AutoConnect. There is an automatic connection between the new and old shapes.
- Utilize the Quick Shapes small toolbar to add a shape. There is an automatic connection between the new and old shapes.
- After choosing the Connector tool, drag a shape from the Basic Flowchart Shapes stencil. There is an automatic connection between the new and old shapes.

Utilize Dynamic Connectors to Connect Flowchart Shapes that Already Exist

Mix and match any of the subsequent ideas:

- Select the Connector tool and drag to create dynamic glue by moving it from one shape's inner to another.
- Drag from the connection point on one shape to the connection point on another using the Connector tool to generate static glue.
- Transfer an AutoConnect arrow (dynamic glue) from one form to another or to a connecting point (static glue).

To Add Text to a Flowchart Shape, Follow these steps

Take one or more of the subsequent actions:

- Select a shape and type text inside it.
- Type text into a form by double-clicking it.
- Select a shape, then hit F2 to input text and switch to edit mode.

Take any of the Following Actions to Exit the Text-Entry Mode:

- Choose any spot outside the editing shape.
- Press the Esc key.

- Select F2.

Understanding Swimlane Diagrams

One disadvantage of flowcharts is that they do not indicate who is responsible for each task and decision. In Chapter 8, "Work with Shape Data," data fields in flowchart shapes can be used to store this information. However, the overall layout or design of a flowchart does not reveal the responsible parties.

A swimlane diagram offers a solution to this problem as an alternative to a flowchart. In a swimlane diagram, each step of the process is placed in a distinct lane, with each lane representing a specific position, function, or department. For example, a swimlane diagram organized by roles might have lanes labeled Flight Attendant, Pilot, and Luggage Handling.

A swimlane diagram is also known as a cross-functional flowchart because it shows how work steps cross functional organizational boundaries. In this context, each swimlane is referred to as a functional band.

Sidebar: Add in Tabs

Certain Visio templates require specific applications to fully demonstrate their capabilities. This applies to Visio add-ins like the cross-functional flowchart template. Cross-functional flowcharts, similar to many add-ins, offer a dedicated tab on the ribbon, as shown in this image.

The Cross-functional Flowchart tab consists of three groups. In the Insert group, you can add a swimlane, a separator, or even a new page.

The Arrange group allows you to adjust the position, direction, and margins of the swimlanes. The Design group offers various design options, the ability to rotate swimlane labels, and a checkbox to display the title bar and swimlane separator.

Swimlane diagrams can be either horizontal or vertical. When starting a new diagram, you can choose the preferred orientation using the Cross-functional Flowchart dialog box shown above. This dialog box appears only the first time you create a swimlane diagram; the orientation you select becomes the default for future diagrams.

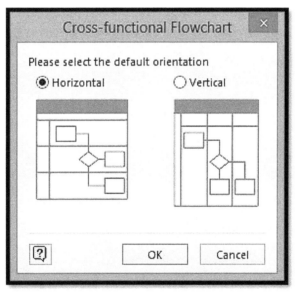

To change the orientation of an existing diagram or set a new default orientation for future diagrams, go to the Orientation menu on the Cross-functional Flowchart add-in tab.

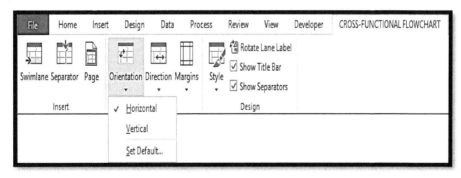

To Adjust the Direction of the Swimlane Diagram

- In the Cross-functional Flowchart section's Organize group, click the Orientation button. Prior to the orientation that is currently set, notice the check mark.
- Select between vertical or horizontal.

To Change the Future Schematics' Orientation

- Choose the Set Default button after selecting the Orientation button.
- Choose Horizontal or Vertical from the Cross-functional flowchart dialog box, then click OK.

Design Swimlane Diagrams

Nobody is assigned to each task in the sample flowchart of a hiring procedure for human resources that was discussed in the previous issue. This section will examine a cross-functional flowchart for a related process to see how the positions of the work steps in the diagram make it easier to grasp responsibilities.

When you select a horizontal orientation for a different process map, the page with your swimlane diagram will be the one that displays.

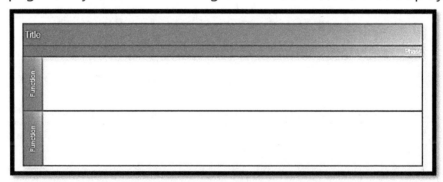

Although a swimlane is a type of Visio shape with distinct attributes, it's essentially just like any other shape. You can perform tasks with it using familiar techniques. For instance, in the sample swimlane diagram provided, the recruiting tasks are distributed among four roles, necessitating the addition of two more swimlanes. These swimlanes should also be labeled with the corresponding role names. For instance, simply dragging a lane from a stencil, just like any other shape, is a swift method to include a lane. In this case, dragging a new swimlane onto the canvas prompts the existing lanes to adjust vertically or horizontally to accommodate the new lane, thanks to the added intelligence in the swimlane diagram framework.

You can input text directly into the lanes or the swimlane structure by selecting the header and typing.

When it comes to adding flowchart shapes to the diagram, you can use any of the methods taught in the "Build flowcharts" section earlier in this chapter. It's worth noting that all techniques for adding dynamic connectors, such as AutoConnect and Quick Shapes, work both within and across swimlane boundaries.

Even as you add shapes across lanes, Dynamic Grid guidelines persistently appear. In this illustration, you can observe familiar guidelines—a double-headed arrow indicating spacing, and horizontal and vertical dashed lines indicating alignment—alongside a new guideline. The dashed line spanning the entire width of a swimlane indicates that the shape within the Recruiter lane is vertically centered within the lane.

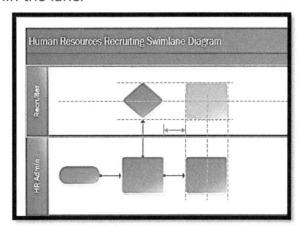

To Integrate a Swimlane into a Schematic

Utilize any of the subsequent actions:

- Click the Swimlane button in the Cross-functional Flowchart tab's Insert group.
- Using the Insert 'Swimlane' Before or Insert 'Swimlane' After option, right-click the header of an already-existing lane.
- Using the Cross-functional Flowchart Shapes stencils, drag a Swimlane shape onto the current lane boundary.
- Move the mouse to the swimlane, then pick the blue insertion triangle at the intersection of two lanes.

Labeling a swimlane Diagram

- Type the desired text in the header that appears above or next to the swimlanes.

To Name a Swimlane

- To enter any text, press the header at one end of the swim lane and type it there.

It is possible to add and connect shapes in a cross-functional flowchart

- Apply any tactics outlined in the steps that follow the "Build flowcharts" of the different participants in this chapter.

Understand BPMN

Business process specialists globally devised the Business Process Model and Notation (BPMN) standard to enable process diagrams to convey more information about a process compared to a traditional flowchart or a swimlane diagram. The primary objective of BPMN is to enhance process communication within a company.

Traditional flowcharts often lack sufficient detail about a procedure for an IT department to develop solutions to support the activities of a business group. BPMN aims to address this gap. While BPMN diagrams can facilitate knowledge transfer for human processes, they are also beneficial for enhancing communication for automated processes. The creators of BPMN utilized standard flowchart designs to ensure that a BPMN diagram remains recognizable.

However, they enhanced these shapes by creating multiple versions of each to provide additional context and significance. As depicted in the images accompanying this and subsequent topics, most BPMN shapes can incorporate one or more icons within them. These additional icons provide crucial information about a process phase to the reader. The BPMN templates in Visio 2016 and 2013 conform to the BPMN 2.0 standard. Visio 2010, the initial version of Visio to introduce a BPMN template, supports BPMN 1.2.

BPMN utilizes four primary types of shapes: Events, Activities, Gateways, and Linking Objects, each featuring various variations. Visio bright shapes prove beneficial in visually representing these shape alterations.

The BPMN 2.0 symbol set comprises the following symbols:

- Three types of events are represented: Start, Intermediate, and End events, depicted as circles with different margins in the top row of the image.

In the bottom row of the image, there is one variation of each event type, shown from left to right: a timed start event, a message-based intermediate event, and an error-triggered end event. In Visio, all six event shapes shown below, along with several other possibilities not depicted, are represented by the same shape.

In drawing tools that lack the versatility of Visio, representing dozens of visual variants like this would require creating dozens of different shapes. The section titled "Design BPMN diagrams" later in this chapter offers a straightforward method for changing the shape across its various incarnations.

- Two types of activities exist: Task and Sub-Process activities, both utilizing the same Visio shape with multiple versions.

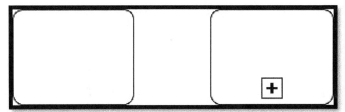

- Six types of gateways exist. Gateways serve to signify decisions and points where process paths diverge or converge. Each gateway variant is represented by a diamond shape.

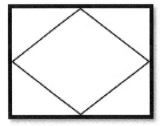

- Three types of connectors

Design BPMN Diagram

The BPMN Basic Shapes template contains the 16 shapes depicted here. However, as noted in the previous topic, most shapes offer one or more shortcut menu options. Therefore, despite the limited stencil, you can create hundreds of variants of these core shapes.

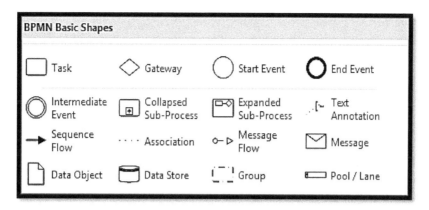

This section covers the techniques for crafting a BPMN diagram. The example provided in this topic demonstrates the design of a theater ticketing procedure, as depicted in the image below. Throughout the process, you'll observe that this is an outdated ticketing process in need of an update—exactly what is addressed in the "Build subprocesses" section that follows.

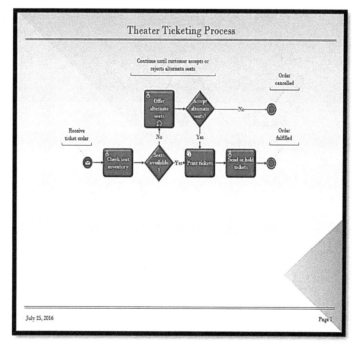

When you initiate a diagram using the BPMN template, the fundamental task of crafting the process map resembles the methods you've previously learned in this chapter with flowcharts and swimlane

127

diagrams. However, distinctions emerge when engaging with the shapes to configure and leverage their BPMN-specific attributes.

Whether you opt for AutoConnect arrows and the Quick Shapes mini toolbar or another method, within minutes, your diagram could resemble this, or if you've chosen to apply themes and effects, it might resemble this.

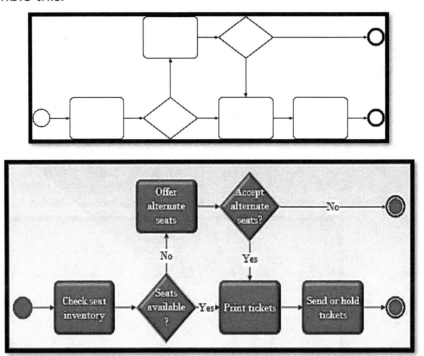

The AutoConnect arrows might not show once you point to the shape to start a BPMN diagram that you've created by dragging a Start Event onto the page. If you zoom in and give it another go, you ought to see the AutoConnect arrows.

BPMN shapes accept text in the same manner as flowchart shapes. As you saw in the flowchart topic previously in this chapter, you can enter text for shapes and labels for outcome pathways, as shown below.

As your drawing page typically has a white background, the text block on a dynamic connection is often invisible. However, in diagrams with a colorful backdrop like the one shown above and those that follow, you might opt to remove the backdrop from the text block. While the method may seem a bit obscure, the simplest option is to utilize the Visio Tell Me feature: select one or more connections, type "format" in the Tell Me box, and then click "**Format Text**." In the Text dialog box that appears, navigate to the Text Block tab, select "None" in the Text Background section, and click **OK**.

The majority of BPMN shapes offer a range of shortcut menu options to convey additional information about the shape. When these values are configured, icons appear on the shapes, enabling the reader to quickly grasp more details about each phase in the process.

For instance, you can indicate that the delivery of a message triggers the start of this operation. By right-clicking the Start Event shape, a cascading menu will appear, allowing you to select "Message."

For the theater ticketing process diagram, utilize the same shortcut menus to change the task type to "**User**" for the "**Check Seat Inventory**" process phase, "**Service**" for the "Print Tickets" process step, and again "User" for the "**Send or Hold Tickets**" process step.

"Offer Alternative Seats" is a looping activity that requires two configuration settings: the task type should be set to "User," and the loop type should be set to "**Standard**."

Certain BPMN shapes can be further annotated using a callout shape. This callout, known as Text Annotation, is available in the BPMN Basic Shapes stencil. When you drag a Text Annotation shape onto the page, you'll see that it includes both a text area and a tail.

Here is the completed sample BPMN diagram, which includes annotations for the Start and End events as well as the "Offer Alternative Seats" loop shape. The annotations "Start" and "Finish" indicate what initiates and concludes the process. The loop's comment specifies the conditions under which it ends.

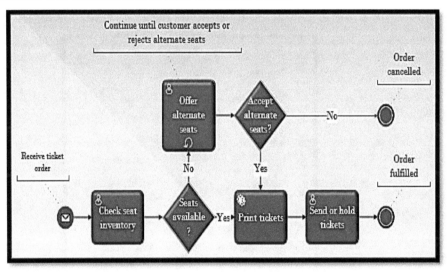

The outdated nature of this diagram should now be evident: the process only permits printing tickets and either delivering them or holding them at the box office. The next section will guide you through establishing a subprocess to update the map.

To be More Specific About the Type of Activities

- Use the flyout menu to pick an entry after right-clicking a task shape and selecting Task Type.

130

To Determine the Type of Loop

- To choose an option from the pop-up menu, right-click a task shape, select Loop.

To Configure the Gateway Type

- To pick an entry from the flyout menu, right-click a gateway form, choose Gateway Type from the flyout menu.

To Set up the Trigger/Result and the Type of Event

- To choose an event shape, right-click on it, choose Event Type, then pick an item from the flyout menu.
- From the flyout menu, choose Trigger/Result by right-clicking an event shape.

To Add a Text Annotation into a BPMN Shape

- Drag a Text Annotation shape onto the page to create it.
- To reach the destination BPMN shape, move the yellow control handle located at the tail of the text annotation shape.

To Make the Text Annotation Shape Larger or Smaller in Size

- Select the callout and drag any of the eight handles to resize.

To Modify the Orientation of a Text Annotation Shape

- Modify the interior of the text annotation shape. The related form is still attached to the tail.

Create Subprocesses

Utilizing a business process raises the possibility of at least one of the following taking place:

- You'll be able to determine which process steps need more detailed explanation.
- Throughout the process, sets of tasks will be mentioned in various situations.

- Some of the effectiveness of your procedure will be lost.
- Your map will become heavy, hard to read, and difficult to keep up with.

A common solution to these problems is to select a group of similar process steps and replace them with a single sub-process symbol. Although you can manually add a new page and cut and paste shapes, Visio Professional offers three buttons on the Process tab that make generating subprocesses much easier.

Using text from the selected shape as its name, "Create New" in Visio generates a new page, labels it, and creates a hyperlink leading to this new page.

"Link To Existing" in Visio creates a link from the selected shape to an existing page of your choice. The destination page can be in the current drawing or another drawing.

Creating a New Subprocess

- Select a subprocess shape, then click the "Create New" button in the Subprocess group on the Process tab.

To link to an existing subprocess

- After selecting a subprocess shape, tap the "Connect to Existing" button.
- Choose the desired page from the menu.

To create a subprocess from existing shapes

- Once at least two forms have been chosen, hit the Create from Selection option.
- Complete the new subprocess shape's text.
- Go to the newly created subprocess page and complete the subprocess's definition.

Summary

In this chapter, we covered a range of topics, from creating flowcharts to selecting templates. You'll gain a deeper understanding of swimlane diagrams, which are better suited for holding much more information.

Chapter 5

Create An Organization Chart

You can manually create reporting relationships in an organization chart by dragging smart org chart shapes onto a page and letting Visio arrange them. Alternatively, you can use the Organization Chart Wizard to point Visio to a data set and let it handle everything automatically. Regardless of the method you choose, Visio offers a wide range of options for customizing your org chart's design, layout, themes, and colors.

This chapter guides you through the steps to create an organization chart using pre-existing data, utilize the Organization Chart Wizard with new data, modify the structure and appearance of an org chart, and insert pictures.

Understanding Organization Charts

The first thing to know is that the Visio organization chart is optimized for hierarchical structures, making it ideal for organizations with a clear boss. However, other organization charts may use matrix or non-hierarchical structures. Despite this, Visio provides efficient tools for creating various types of organization charts.

Reviewing the New Features

Visio 2013 introduced striking aesthetic updates to the ten-year-old org chart solution, which were further enhanced in Visio 2016. The most significant aesthetic impact came with the addition of styles to org charts. Visio now offers 10 different styles, each with six custom chart shapes. You'll find that some representations of your company's employees are more suitable than others. Visio simplifies the process of exploring different options by allowing you to switch between styles with a single click.

The Visio org charts have an enhanced appearance due to two additional elements that were retained from Visio 2013.

Among these features are:

- The stylized form: these are decorated and themed.
- Automatic photo import is also supported by the organization chart shape.

They stand out more in the organization chart thanks to the add-on software. As with the others, you may also view the organizational charts. It's located on the ribbon in Visio.

The Org Chart tab still contains a number of commonly used Visio controls, including those for arranging and spacing shapes. Visio 2016 includes a tab with buttons that you may use to import and manage images as well as take use of styles.

Visio 2016 offers two organizational chart designs in the Business section. Other than the above, both templates share the same features and stencils: The Organization Chart Wizard opens on the same blank page as the Organization Chart, but it also displays the wizard's initial page, which walks you through the process of making a chart. An organization chart can be manually created by starting with a blank sheet.

Utilize Organizational Chart Templates

In the Business section of Visio, you can find two organizational chart templates. Both templates offer the same capabilities and stencils, except for one distinction: the Organization Chart Wizard template begins with a blank page and also presents the first page of a wizard, which assists you in creating a chart. On the other hand, the Organization Chart template starts with a blank page, allowing you to construct an org chart manually.

Manually Building of Organization Charts

If you accidentally select the Organization Chart Wizard, there's no need to worry; simply cancel it and proceed without it. Likewise, if you opt for the manual templates but decide to use the wizard, you can access it by choosing the Import option on the Org Chart tab.

It's useful to know how easy it is to construct org charts manually, even if the Organization Chart Wizard will be covered in later courses. Fortunately, Visio still does a good deal of the heavy lifting when you manually create an organizational chart. For example, dragging an Executive shape to the top of the page and then dragging other shapes will quickly produce an image of the reporting hierarchy.

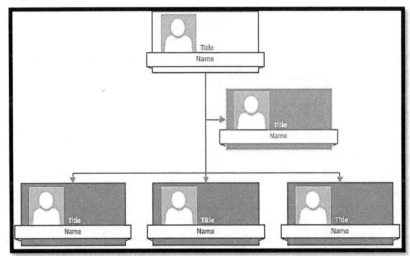

Once a shape has been dragged to the page, you can decide that it belongs to a different shape type without having to delete and replace it. Many techniques to alter the type are provided in the processes that follow this page.

With the Organization Chart Shapes stencil, you can easily add three employees to the chart at once thanks to the special shape called Three Positions. In addition, the stencil has a form named Many Shapes. When dragging this shape over an existing org chart shape, it would be helpful if you first selected the shape type and then indicated how many of that sort you want to add to the chart.

Adding titles and subtitles to the chart is straightforward; simply enter them twice on the shape. To input a title, click anywhere on the shape, and to input a name, click the name box. You can expand the chart by adding more shapes on top of existing ones to indicate the required reporting linkages, possibly creating a similar chart.

The background of the executive, manager, and vacancy shapes are respectively white, dark, and prominent, with the vacancy shape located at the lower right corner of the image standing out from the other shapes. Because of their pleasing qualities, these four categories of shapes are easily recognized. The default organization chart shape style (Belt) in the picture, however, does not distinguish between assistants, consultants, and non-managerial positions.

Although the forms are the identical, the only method to differentiate assistants such as Deedee Spiros and Jason Robinson from positions and consultants is by their physical positioning, which is offset to the right under their respective bosses.

To Create Organization Chart Manually

- Provide the backstage viewpoint.
- Select New from the left pane of the Backstage view.
- Choose Categories from the New page, then click on the Business thumbnail. Once that's done, double-click the

Organization Chart template (not the Organization Chart Wizard template).

- Drag and drop a form that represents the top tier of your company onto the page, such as an Executive Belt or even a Manager Belt form.
- Beneath the top-level form, add more shapes that reflect the tiers of the organization.
- Keep adding shapes to each tier until your business is completely covered.
- Put names and titles on the forms.

To add three position forms at once, drag the three job shapes onto an executive or management shape that already exists.

To Add a Variety of Shapes of any Kind

- To access the Add Many Shapes dialog box, drag the Numerous shapes form onto an existing executive or management shape, or onto an empty space on the drawing page.

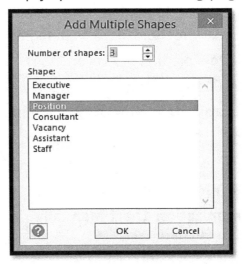

- In the Add Multiple Shapes dialog box, you can specify the number of shapes you want to add by entering or selecting a number.

- Select a shape type, then click OK in the Shape section of the Add Multiple Shapes dialog box.

To modify a shape's position type on a drawing page, first choose the Change Position Type option from the context menu of any org chart shape, then select the desired position's name.

Utilize Existing Data to Generate an Organizational Chart

Visio provides a wizard that can generate the organizational chart for you if your company's information is already available in electronic form.

To get started, you can use information from any of these directories:

o An Excel workbook

o A database system, such as Microsoft Access, SQL Server, or another database

o A Microsoft Exchange Server directory

o An application that generates text files or Excel workbooks for exporting personnel data

When creating an org chart from existing data, only two key pieces of information about each employee are needed: the employee's identity and the name of the person they report to. However, as shown in the figure, you can include more information. Depending on your preferences for the chart, you may choose to provide additional information beyond the required data.

- You may decide whether to create a chart utilizing existing data or to add data employing the wizard on the main page of an organization chart wizard, as shown in this figure. The wizard pages that result from using existing data are shown in the remaining sections of this article.

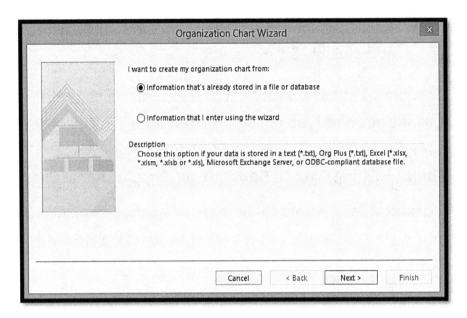

- On the second wizard page, you may select the type of data source to use.
- If you choose a text, plus (*.txt), or an Excel file as the data source, you may indicate where you wish the file to be located on the subsequent wizard page.

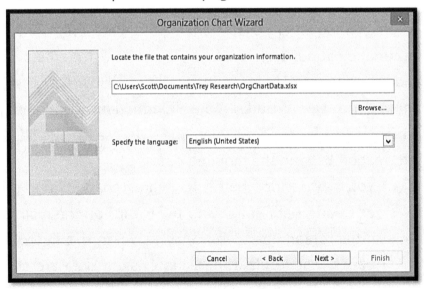

- When you open the data source with the wizard, you'll encounter the following:

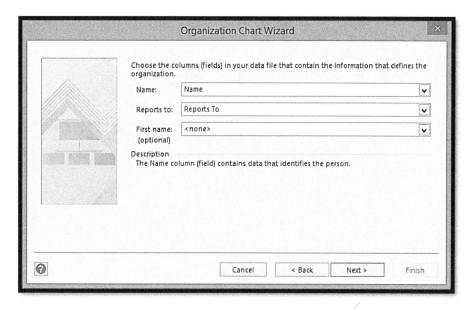

- This is where you can map a field from your data to the Reports field and another to the org chart name field. If there is a separate field in the data for the employee first names, you can indicate that.

- You may select the fields from the data that you would like Visio to display on each org chart shape on the fifth wizard page.

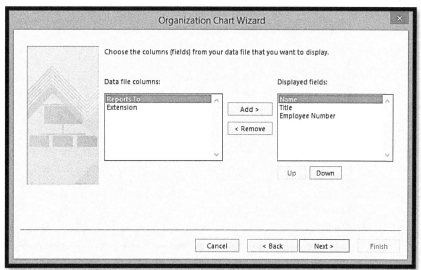

- Although this wizard page looks similar to the one before it, it has a different and unrelated goal. For every org chart shape on this page, you select the fields you wish to preserve as shape data from the data source. You can create reports and use the data for various purposes without having to visit the original data source by storing it inside shapes.

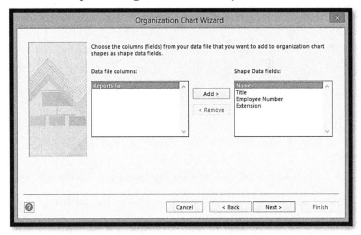

The following page was introduced in Visio 2013. Here, you may decide whether to import a photograph into the org chart. If you opt for this, you'll need to specify the location for the photos and provide instructions to the wizard on how to match the photo files with the employees.

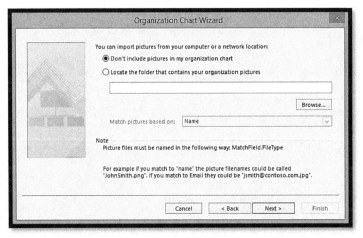

- On the wizard's final page, you must make the following decision:

- Whether Visio will determine how much information to display on each page, or if you will.

If you choose to complete the assignment yourself, you will be prompted with a page where you can make changes to the page's content.

If you let Visio to create the pages, you can point to the top shape on the first page to tell it where to start. Visio is instructed to select the top shape as the one that reports to no one else by selecting the Top Executive> option.

As an alternative, you may select a specific person by clicking the arrow and any name on your list.

- If employee shapes ought to be connected between pages

If the manager's direct reports don't fit inside the page with the manager, the wizard will relocate the manager and the manager's shape to a different page. This option causes Visio to generate a hyperlink between duplicate manager shapes.

- If the shapes of the employees should match up on different pages.

If manager shapes have been duplicated, as shown in the previous bullet point, you can select this box to instruct Visio to edit one form only if the other is modified.

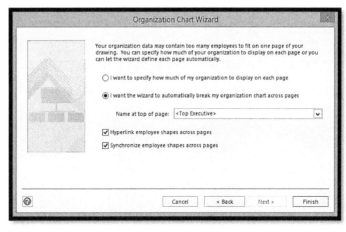

There's a lot of labor involved with this wizard. Even so, you could find that the default layout isn't optimal for your needs. We will walk you through the processes to change the organization chart later in this chapter.

To Initiate the Organization Chart Wizard

Select an option from the following list:

- o Choose Categories, Business, and then double-click the Organization Chart Wizard icon on the New page.
- o Tap the Import button located in the Organization Data section of the Org Chart tab while the organizational chart is open.

Utilize the Organization Chart Wizard with Updated Information and Visual Design

Should the data for your company not be in a Visio-readable format, you can still use the wizard. The Organization Chart Wizard can help by creating a file, such as an Excel worksheet, into which it's possible to paste or enter your data.

The organization chart wizard pauses the moment you create a workbook or text file and doesn't stop until you close it. A dialog box with the files excel.exe or notepad.exe will appear if you don't close the file.

Using the Data you Submitted to Subsequently Generate Organization Data Charts

- o To begin, launch the organization chart wizard. Next, navigate to the first page and choose the data using the wizard.
- o From the wizard page that follows, choose Excel or delimited text.
- o Navigate to or enter the location of the data file you wish to store on the same wizard screen.

- Select Next. After that, a dialog box appears with instructions for you to input the data over the data sample.
- Hit OK to close the dialog box and complete the remaining pages of the Organization Chart Wizard, allowing Visio to generate your org chart after you have entered your data.

Or

After you enter your data, hit OK to exit the wizard, close the dialog box, launch it again, and point it to your completed data file.

Modify the Layout and Appearance

You can alter the look of your organization chart in a variety of ways by utilizing the extensive set of enhancements included in Visio 2013. Furthermore, Visio redesigned the Org Chart tab in 2016 and has since enhanced the usability of the org chart customization tools.

The four groups on the Org Chart tab that this piece covers are Layout, Arrange, Shapes, and Images. The subject matter also demonstrates the influence of Visio themes on organization charts. If you reformat an Organization Chart Wizard-created org chart using the aforementioned procedures, be aware that if you later import your data to update your org chart, all formatting will be lost. Each time you launch the Visio wizard, a fresh organizational chart is produced.

Modify the layout

To change the shape's location on the page, use the Layout group located inside the chart tab.

An organization chart can be significantly changed by choosing any one of the eighteen preset layouts. The chart's shapes' relative positions and spacing are changed by each setup. Upon clicking the Layout button, a menu containing multiple layout options displays.

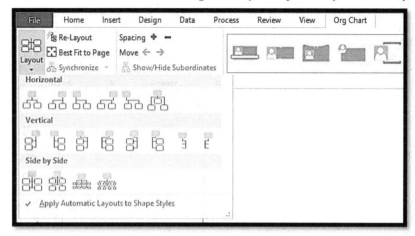

If you click the box at the bottom of the menu labeled Apply Automatic Layouts To Shape Styles, Visio adjusts the org chart layout every time a style is applied. If you uncheck this option, you may switch styles without changing the layout. If you manually adjust any org chart shape's size or location, your diagram can have gaps or overlapping forms. The remedy is simple and can be found in the organization chart add-in: simply press the Re-Layout icon to restore proper spacing.

Another useful tool in the Layout area is the Best Fit To Page symbol. To free up more space on the current page, press this button to move the entire organizational chart.

To Modify the Design of an Organizational Chart Page

- In the Org Chart tab, hit the Layout button located under the Layout group.
- Select either the Horizontal, Vertical, or Side by Side radio button.

To Change the Layout of an Organizational Chart Page Completely or in Part

- Select Arrange Subordinates after selecting Subordinates from the context menu of any shape that has subordinates.
- In the Arrange Subordinates dialog box, hit OK after selecting the relevant Horizontal, Vertical, or Side-by-Side boxes.

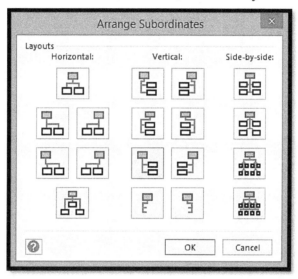

- To create an organizational chart with all the appropriate shapes, sizes, and placements, choose the Re-Layout button in the Org Chart tab under the Layout group.
- Select "Best Fit to Page" from the Layout category if you wish to center the org chart on the page.

Arrange the Shapes

To alter the shapes' vertical spacing and placement in your organization chart, utilize the Move and Spacing options in the Arrange group. The Move icons function more locally, but it's vital to remember that the Spacing icons impact every shape on the page. If you select a management or executive shape, then that person and all subordinates will move; otherwise, the Move buttons will simply move the selected shape if you choose a form without subordinates.

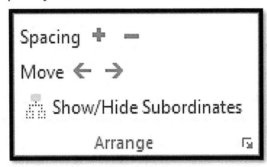

It is also possible to hide areas of the organization chart that list a management or executive's subordinates. The manager or executive form that has hidden subordinates will show an icon in the lower-right corner if you want to hide it. This indicator indicates that there are hidden subordinates.

To Change the Vertical Separation between the Shapes

- Locate and press the Raise the Spacing (+) or Decrease the Spacing (-) button in the Org Chart tab's Arrange group.

Moving a Single Shape

- Select a form devoid of offspring.
- Select either the Move Left/Up (Image) or Move Right/Down (Image) button.

Reorganize a Collection of Shapes

- Select a form together with children.
- Select the "Picture" button.

Subordinates can be Shown or Hidden

- Choose a shape with the children in it.
- Select the option to Show or Hide Subordinates.

- Use the Hide Subordinates or Show Subordinates buttons when you right-click a shape that has subordinates to hide or show them.

Modify the Shape and Appearance

The Shapes group's buttons, as seen in the image, allow you to change the appearance of your organization chart. The most obvious changes are caused by the 10 buttons in the format of an organizational chart, each with a different form design and set of layout principles. Since altering your look is so easy, you can try out looks that range from professional to fantasy.

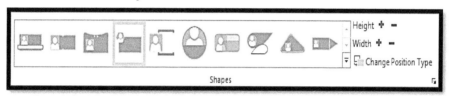

You can tell Visio to swap the shape but not the layout if you don't want this, perhaps because you have already invested a lot of work in customizing the arrangement. Visio typically changes the shape arrangement when you transition to a different type of organizational chart.

Side bar: The Names are Constantly Changing

In the Organization Chart Shapes stencil, the name of the current org chart style appears in each of the six main shape names. The names of the shapes might thus have changed since your last organizational chart project.

Since Belt is the default design, this is how the upper portion of the stencil looks whenever you create a new organizational chart.

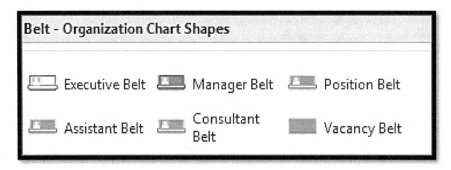

Whenever you choose a new style icon in the Shapes group, the stencil and shape titles update. In order to display additional data on a shape or remove unused space, the Shapes group also contains buttons for adjusting the height and width of organizational chart shapes.

Changing the Appearance of the Organization Chart

- Select a style icon from the ten available options under the Org Chart tab's Shapes category.

Or

- If the style you want to use is not immediately apparent, hit the More button in the lower-right corner of the style section to display a gallery on the Styles menu.
- Select one of the 10 available style icons.

To Change the Layout of an Organizational Chart But Not Its

Structure

- Select the style button, Hit **Ctrl+Z** to undo the changes, and then tap the Undo button again to change the layout and style. The style change can be undone twice, and the layout can be undone once.) Visio arranges the changes into two separate blocks. This is why it functions.

To Modify the Widths or Heights of One or More Shapes

- Select a shape or shapes.

- Tap the (+) or (-) buttons under the Shapes category to change the height or width, respectively.

Working with the Images

After constructing the organizational chart, you may add photographs to it, as you will discover later in this chapter. If an organizational chart already exists, you can add one or more photographs to it by using the Insert button in the Image group.

The Change and Delete buttons within the Picture group allow you to swap out or remove images.

The Show/Hide button can be used to make the photographs or placeholders for the pictures appear or disappear. For each of the ten org chart designs, the preset display includes a placeholder image; however, if you don't have any photos, you can use the Hide option. With a single click of the Show/Hide button, the image on the left is transformed into a more visually appealing one on the right.

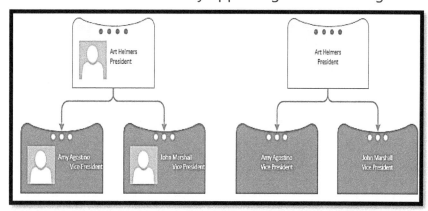

This is how to update an existing organizational chart with a photo.

- Select a few shapes for organizational charts.
- To input several photos, choose the Insert button and pick Picture or Many photos from the Picture group here on the Org Chart tab.

Change a Picture in the Shape of an Organizational Chart

- Select just one form.
- Select the Image group's Change button.
- After selecting an image file, hit Open.

How to Delete Pictures or Picture Placeholders

- Select a shape or shapes.
- On the Org Chart tab, select the Erase button located under the Image group.

Add Themes

The Visio themes on the Design tab and the buttons on the Org Chart tab can be used to modify org charts. To get the right look, you may utilize themes to add different hues, effects, and decorations.

Import Photographs as you Create Organization Charts

Visio 2013 was the first edition of the program to support the simultaneous import of several photographs. The feature is still included in Visio 2016 and later iterations. It was possible to import only one image at a time in previous versions. If you make an organizational chart with information from an Excel spreadsheet or database, you can import images from the folder on a computer or the server. If you create your org chart using data from Microsoft Exchange Server, you can import the same pictures that users use in their Microsoft Outlook profiles.

The trick to having photos automatically added as you create an org chart is on the first page of the Organization Chart Wizard. You can locate the folder containing your photo after selecting from the dialog to find the Folder Which Has Your Organization Pictures. In addition, you must specify to the wizard which data field to utilize in order to match the org chart shapes with the image files. In accordance with the list, you may select the default Name or a different field in Match Pictures.

Whenever you add images into an org chart in Visio, it automatically adjusts and repositions each image to fit as tightly as possible inside the form's picture frame. In general, Visio should be placed appropriately. However, you may from time to time trim, edit, or change a photo in some other way. You can accomplish this by first selecting the image and then using the tools on the Format tool tab of the Image Tool.

Using Images in the Organizational Chart Created with the Wizard

- Assemble the photo folder by giving each file a name that corresponds to a database column.
- Launch the Organization Chart Wizard.
- On the photos page of a wizard, tap Find the folder containing the pictures of your organization, then select the folder containing the pictures.
- Using the list as a guide, select an alternate match location, or leave the Name selected in the match photos.
- Finish the wizard.

To Crop or Make an Edit of a Photo Inside the Org chart

- Select the photo after choosing the shape containing it.

- Next, select the appropriate tool from the picture tools format menu and modify the photo.
- To get out of the edit mode, choose any area of the picture.

Summary

We studied organization charts in further detail in this chapter. We concentrate on the less common use of Visio, which is for creating a chart with personnel data to show the organizational structure. Moreover, their picture is included in the chart. We study the practical applications of Visio in the real world.

Chapter 6

Apply Style, Color and Themes

Certain Visio diagrams are simple and simply serve to represent a functional or mechanical concept. Still, a lot of diagrams provide information and sometimes even narrate a story.

Regardless of the category your diagram falls into, there are a number of techniques you may use to enhance both its aesthetic appeal and informative value. Coloring a diagram's inside shapes and lines is a common place to start. Because choosing a unique yet complementary color scheme can be difficult, Fast Styles and Visio themes were created. For those occasions when you want something a little bit different, they provide skillfully designed color schemes and variations on the main theme.

It doesn't matter if you design your own palette or use Visio themes—you may still apply certain colors, gradients, and patterns to specific shapes.

This chapter covers the following topics: using effects and Quick Styles, applying preset themes and variants to pages or entire diagrams, aligning and spacing shapes, and filling shapes with solid gradients. Use the Format Painter, pattern fills, and applying colors and patterns to particular forms.

Align and Space shapes

One part of creating an appropriate Visio diagram is making the content easy to understand and learn from. You can greatly assist your reader by getting rid of distractions like forms that are almost perfectly aligned and lines that cross pointlessly.

Even though we have already covered everything, it would still be crucial to go over it again. From some of the previous chapters, you know that the Dynamic Grid, AutoConnect, rulers, and guidelines can help you create a tidy diagram. You are also aware that forms can be manually pushed and shifted into more exact positions. We will walk you through these in the upcoming chapter items.

Align shapes

These shapes will serve as an example for us.

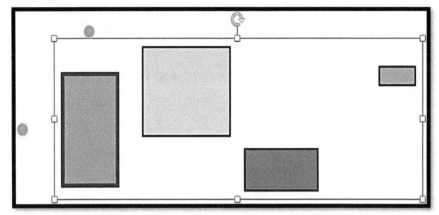

Sidebar: What is in Front?

Even though Visio is a two-dimensional drawing application, you must realize that every design involves a third dimension in order to fully utilize the features presented in this chapter.

Positioning the shapes on a Visio drawing page will show you where they are in relation to the X- and Y-axes, respectively, in both vertical and horizontal directions. It is less evident that each shape is likewise positioned along the Z-axis. The Z-axis placement of a shape can be thought of as its distance from the page's edge.

The Z-order of a shape, or its relative location on the Z-axis, can be seen when shapes on a page overlap; particular shapes appear to be "in front of" or "behind" other shapes.

Visio tracks the position of every shape on the Z-axis even when they are not stacked on top of one another. The first shape you put on a page is at the back, and each subsequent form you add is automatically one step ahead of the previous one.

If you aren't sure, try the following:

- As you arrange the three shapes on the drawing paper, make sure they are not in contact with one another.
- Drag the second shape that fell to encompass the third component. It is visible that it appears behind the third form.
- Shift the first form to partially surround the second and third shapes. After the other two shapes, the initial shape keeps appearing in the Z-order. Any form or set of shapes can have its Z-order altered by using the Bring To Front and Send To Back buttons.

Utilizing the Home tab and the small toolbar buttons, shapes can be moved fully in a single direction. The buttons feature menus that contain the Bring Forward and Send Backward commands, which can be used to move shapes gradually. The shape that is in front of you is usually the anchor shape. To pick every shape, use Ctrl+A.

Usually, Z-order is the basis on which Visio selects the anchor. The anchor is frequently the shape that is closest to the back when multiple shapes are chosen using a bounding box. In either case, you can permanently modify the anchor's shape for a single selection by adjusting the Z-order with the Send Backward and Send Forward commands.

Temporarily overriding the Z-order, you may designate a specific shape to be the anchor by selecting it and then the other forms. The process for the left, center, and appropriate alignment will result in the following if you choose every rectangle in the above list.

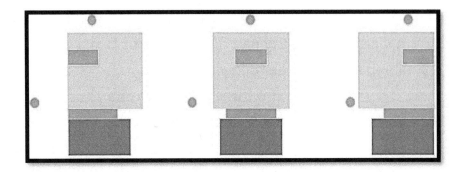

However, as can be seen above, the shapes are moved vertically if you employ the aligned top, aligned middle, and aligned bottom operations.

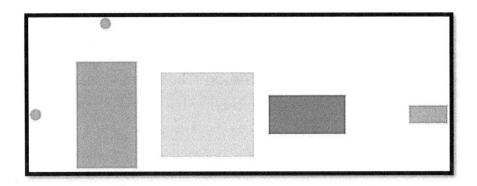

To Arrange Shapes with Proportion to the Left, Center or Right of the Anchor shape

- Choose Align Left, Align Center, or Align Right after clicking the Align button in the Arrange group of the Home tab.

In order to arrange shapes inside, outside or above the anchor shape

- After selecting the Align button, select the Top, Middle, or Bottom alignment option.

Space and Oriented shapes

Changing the spacing between shapes in a diagram is a useful technique for enhancing its presentation. A ruler, a guide, or even the

Dynamic Grid can be of use, but in many cases, the Position button will do just fine.

For example, the distribute functions ensure that, for a set of shapes on either the horizontal or vertical axis, the inter-shape spacing remains constant. Using our sample shape as an example, select Distribute horizontally from the positions menu to observe what happens.

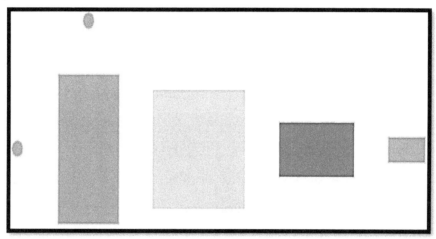

Moreover, you may use the Position button to rotate and flip individual forms or the entire diagram.

To move shapes away from page breaks or instruct Visio not to place shapes on page breaks in a diagram if the drawing page spans several printing pages, use the Position menu's choices. Both options help keep forms from splitting if you want to print the diagram on multiple sheets of paper.

This is how Shapes are Distributed

- Select a minimum of three shapes.
- Choose to Distribute Horizontally or Vertically after clicking the Position button in the Arrange group of the Home tab.

To Turn or Flip Shapes

1. To rotate shapes, click the Positions button, choose Rotate forms from the menu that displays, and then choose between Rotate and Flip.

Organizing Shapes to Avoid a Page Break

- Under Position, select Move off Page Breaks.

Automatically Align and Arrange shapes

Even more powerful automatic alignment and spacing features in Visio allow you to completely redesign a page with just two clicks. Similar to the align and space capabilities covered in the preceding sections, the auto align and space are also quite useful.

This is the Method for Automatically Spacing shapes

- Choose Auto Align after clicking the Align button in the Arrange group on the Home tab.

Organizing Shapes Automatically

- On the Home tab, choose the Arrange group, then click the Position button and choose Auto Space.

Shapes will Align and Space Themselves Automatically

- After selecting the Align button, select the Auto Align and Space button.

Understand Concepts of Themes

With themes and several related Visio features, a diagram's overall appearance can be changed. While some themes utilize bright colors and adorned shapes with glows, reflections, shadows, and other special effects, others use simple shape patterns with minimal color or embellishment.

One of the themes' best features is how simple it is to use. Just tap the thumbnail of the theme you want to use after pointing to any theme in the gallery to see a live preview. There are many different types of themes available, but they're not the only way to enhance your diagram's aesthetic appeal.

The Visio diagram design hierarchy consists of the subsequent four levels:

- **Themes**: They consist of shape matrices, coordinated color palettes, font styles, and visual effects.
- **Variants**: are collections of four variations on a theme, each using different color schemes and shape patterns while maintaining the theme's essential elements.
- **Effect Visual**: are collections of four variations on a theme, each using different color schemes and shape patterns while maintaining the theme's essential elements.
- **Quick style**: sets of color and style combinations, ranging from subtle to dramatic, that can be applied to particular forms and yet maintain the essential elements of the theme and variation you've chosen.

Among its features is a color palette for each theme that includes primary and accent colors. You will find more information about the color palette and a list of specific Visio colors in the section later in this chapter titled "Use solid, gradient, and pattern fills." Hundreds of Visio masters have been updated to reflect the Visio 2016 theming ideas. Sub-shapes with different accent colors within a theme are found in many revised masters. When employing monochromatic themes, the forms have a unified appearance. However, themes with different accent colors might result in visually striking diagram details.

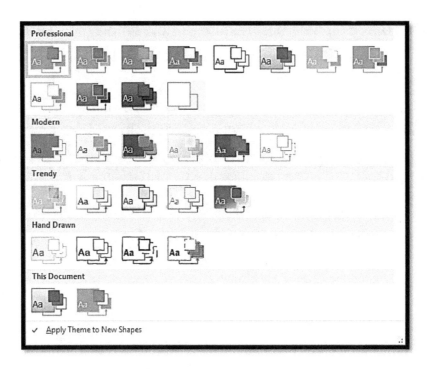

The Themes gallery under the Design tab has 26 themes and a No Theme option. The themes are grouped into four categories: Hand-drawn, professional, trendy and modern

Sidebar: Hand-drawn Themes

Have you ever wanted to show a diagram to a group of people so they could offer feedback, but you were worried it wouldn't look perfect? You can use the intriguing range of themes that Visio 2016 offers to let your viewers know that the drawing remains a work in progress.

The flow charts in the following image can be compared.

The graphic on the left, featuring the Whisp theme, appears to thoughtfully represent a business's process. In contrast, the one on the right, utilizing the Marker theme from the Hand Drawn section of the Themes collection, encourages viewers to help sketch out and develop the process.

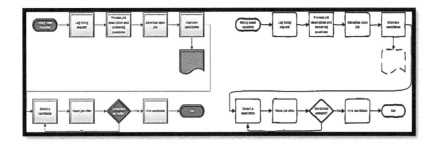

Similarly, examine the professional diagram on the left here.

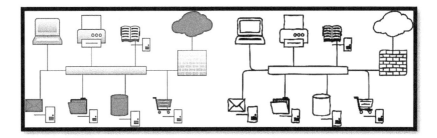

Add Themes and Variants

Visio has many updated shapes, some of which you may see in the figures in the next sections, including forms for office furniture. The furniture forms offer a great deal of aesthetic variety even in the absence of themes. The sections that follow demonstrate how changing the theme or variation could affect the appearance of your diagrams.

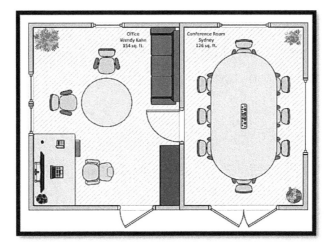

Select Themes and Variants

In the upper left corner of the image above, we applied the shade theme. We get a monochrome vibe from it. Next, notice the whisp motif in the upper right corner, where the shape's accent colors are more noticeable.

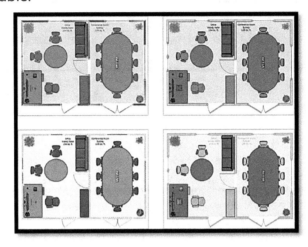

The sofa shape from the Office Furniture stencil remains brown due to a recognized issue, regardless of the theme or variant. It is likely that a later release will address this issue.

Variants add even more visual uniqueness. In the image above, on the left, examine the two different workplace layouts. Both use the Shade theme; however, Variation 2 is used in the lower photo. The seats are the same color as the walls, entrance, tables, and plants, which are all various colors. The image on the right, Variation 4, has an identical subject to the photographs on the left, but a completely different color scheme.

Applying a Theme

Select one of the following actions from the Design tab's Themes category:

- Hit the image to select the preferred theme.

- Utilize the up/down arrows located at the right end of the gallery to navigate between the different themes. Next, select the theme that you want.
- Tap the More icon and choose your preferred theme to browse the Themes gallery.

Adding Themes on Each Diagram Page

- Right-click the thumbnail of the preferred theme and select Apply to All Pages from the context menu.

You Must Apply the Themes From this Page one More

- After right-clicking on the thumbnail of the preferred theme, select Apply to Current Page from the context menu.

Personalize Themes and Variants

- On the Design tab, select the preferred variation by tapping on it in the Variants group.

To Remove the Current Page's Theme

- Select More to view the Themes gallery. Next, select the No Theme graphic located at the Professional section's bottom.

To Take Motifs out Of Selected shapes

- Turn off the Allow Themes check box on the Shape Styles group's more button on the Home tab.

To Restrict the Use of Themes in any Future Works

- Hit the More button to view the Themes gallery. Next, make sure the box next to "**Apply Theme to New Shapes**" is unchecked.

Personalizing Themes ad Variants

- Even if you included a theme in your diagram, you have no reason to cease looking into other themes.

Any theme/variant combination can be changed to produce a custom color palette and style, as demonstrated below:

Colors, You may select an existing color scheme or build your own palette by selecting the option to build New Theme Colors at the bottom of the Colors gallery. If you would like to create your own set of colors, Visio presents you with a dialog box.

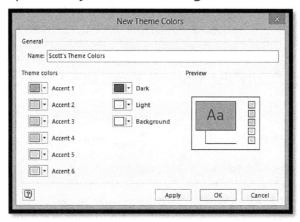

Accent colors, font colors for light and dark fills, and the background color of the entire design can all be chosen here. Whenever you create custom theme colors in Visio, this section of the Colors gallery displays your color scheme in the Custom section. You can also select from samples of pre-made color schemes in the identical figure.

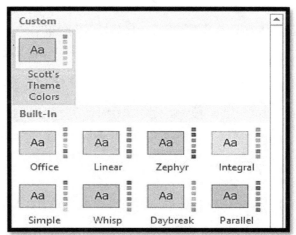

Effects: One of the pre-installed theme effects is yours to select.

Connectors: Additionally, any of the 26 styles can be applied to the dynamic connector.

Embellishment: The level of ornamentation is adjustable. It would be beneficial if you kept in mind that not all forms require adornment, therefore changing the embellishment's setting could not even make a difference.

To replicate a personalized theme between two Visio drawings, copy and paste the first design's shape containing the theme into the second. Even when the form is removed, the theme will still be there. Your duplicate theme won't show up in the Themes gallery, but any custom color sets you make will show up in the Custom section of the Colors gallery.

To Customize Different Colors

- Hit the More button on the Variants group of the Design tab to navigate to Colors in the Variants gallery.
- Decide on the preferred color palette.

Personalize the Effects

- Choose your preferred effect by clicking Effects in the Variants gallery and opening it.

To Alter the Connector style.

- Go to the Variants gallery, click Connectors, then pick the connector type that you want.

To Adjust the Degree of Embellishment

- Choose the appropriate degree of decoration by selecting Embellishment from the Variants gallery.

Utilize Effects and Quick styles

Once you have used themes and variants to give your diagram the correct general appearance, you can use effects and Quick Styles to add extra intricacy or to highlight one or more specific forms in your design.

Highlight Shapes with Effects

In Visio, you may apply six different effects: glows, shadows, bevels, soft edges, and 3-D rotation. One of the six preset effects can be chosen, or you can modify specific elements of each effect. If you've used effects in Microsoft PowerPoint, you might be familiar with this list because both Visio and PowerPoint offer a comparable selection of effects.

The Flowchart's Shapes are Angled

The item at the left end of the bottom row has a golden glow coming from   it.

It is possible to apply effects in two different ways, however the two approaches differ greatly. Unlike the Effects button in the Shape Styles group on the Home tab, which only gives you access to preset effects, the Format Shape task pane lets you fine-tune every aspect of each effect.

For the Effects page of the Format Shape task pane to open

Select one or more shapes, then make your choice from the alternatives below.

- On the Home tab, hit the dialog box launcher located under the Shape Styles group to access the Format Shape task pane. Select the Effects button situated at the task window's top.

- Choose an effect type from the six available options after clicking the Effects button in the Shape Styles group of the Home tab. Click Settings at the bottom of the menu.

To Put the Outcome into Practice

Select a choice from the list below after deciding on one or more shapes.

- From within the Shape Styles group, pick the Effects button and point to one of the six effect categories to choose the appropriate effect.
- On the Format Shape task pane's Effects page, select the name of the preferred effect and enter the desired values.

To Modify a shape's Influence

- In the Format Shape task pane, choose the name of the effect you want to change, and then make the required changes.

To Eliminate Effects from Shapes

- Navigate to the Shape Styles group, click the effects button, point to the desired effect, and then choose no, where "" is the effect's name that you wish to remove.

Embellish shapes with Quick styles

Just as themes offer an organized collection of design choices for a whole page, Quick Styles offer predesigned sets of visual effects for a selection of shapes. Visio provides two Quick Styles galleries that you can use to achieve the same outcome.

The two sections of the Quick Styles gallery provide the following options:

- Four different styles

- There is a six-by-seven matrix with possibilities for colors and styles that match the theme. The rows offer style changes that range from subtle to spectacular, and the matrix columns give variations with numbers ranging from one to seven.

To Easily Incorporate A Style into One or More Shapes

Select a choice from the list below.

- In the Shape Styles group of the Home tab, hit the **More button** to select a thumbnail from the Variant Styles or Theme Styles section of the Quick Styles gallery.
- Press the right mouse button to select the shape or shapes. Select a thumbnail by selecting the Styles button on the small toolbar, located in the Variant Styles or Theme Styles section of the gallery.

To Modify the Quick Styles

- Navigate to the Quick styles collection and select a different thumbnail.

Add Solid Gradient and Pattern Fills

- While themes, variants, and effects provide an incredible range of design possibilities, there are some situations where the essentials are sufficient, such as incorporating color or pattern into a shape.
- To do these activities, choose a color using Visio's color picker. However, themes and variations influence your choice of hue even in this instance. Theme Colors, Variant Colors, Standard Colors, and Recent Colors are the four groups into which each choice is separated.

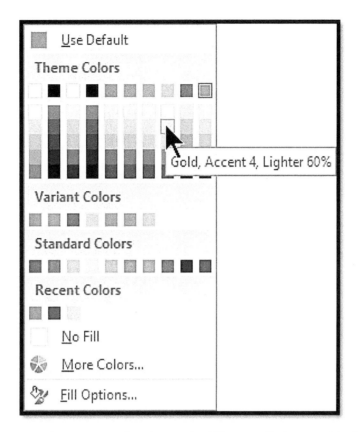

Whenever you choose a color from the Theme Colors or Variant Colors box, the fill inside your shape will vary every time a new theme is applied. If you select your form from the Standard Colors or Recent Colors box, or if you choose More Colors, themes will no longer affect its color.

If you choose to work with the color picker's Theme Colors area, it's helpful to know how it's organized.

What you should know is as follows:

Column: The columns in the Theme Colors section are White, Black, Light, and Dark, arranged from left to right, and then there are six accent colors, denoted as Accent 1 through Accent 6.

171

Row: The primary color of every column is displayed in the row at the top. You will observe three lighter and two darker tones of each hue in the next five rows.

To Achieve Visibility of the Color Picker

Select a choice from the list below.

- On the Home menu, select the Fill button located under the Shape Styles category.
- Click and hold a shape. Point at the Styles button on the little toolbar to select Fill.

To Enable the Format shape plane to be seen

Select a choice from the list below.

- Click the color selector to open it, then choose Fill Options.
- Use the right-click menu to select Format Shape after selecting a shape.
- Open the color selector, then click More Colors to bring up the color dialog box.

Try one of the Following methods to fill in areas with a solid color:

- Hit the matching button to select a color from the Theme Colors, Variant Colors, Standard Colors, or Recent Colors category.
- To choose a desired color, choose the Standard tab in the Colors dialog box.
- After launching the Colors dialog box and selecting the Custom tab, move the tint slider to the desired color in the Colors pane.
- Open the Colors dialog box, choose the Custom tab, select RGB or HSL from the Color model menu, and then type values to select the desired color.
- In the Format Shape task box, pick Solid fill. Next, opt for one of the above-described methods and the Fill Color button.

Select a Transparency value (optional)

Use one of these gradient fill techniques to apply it:

- Select a color from the Theme Colors, Variant Colors, Standard Colors, or Recent Colors categories first by clicking the matching button to launch the color picker.
- Go to the Standard tab in the Colors dialog box to select the required color.
- In the Colors pane, adjust the tinting slider to the necessary value after choosing the Custom tab to open the Colors dialog box.
- Choose RGB or HSL from the Color model menu, enter the Colors dialog box, click the Custom tab, then type values to select the color you want to use.
- Select the Fill Color button and one of the aforementioned ways after selecting Solid fill in the Format Shape task box.

Select a Value for Transparency (not necessary)

Add Line Colors and Patterns

There are numerous theme and variant possibilities for the styles and colors of the lines. Just as you may apply certain colors and patterns to two-dimensional forms, you may also modify lines and dynamic connectors.

The majority of line alterations affect the lines you draw between shapes and the border lines encircling two-dimensional shapes, with very few exceptions. (The "Customize themes and variants" part of the previous chapter noted one exception.) The techniques for changing the appearance of lines are very similar to those covered in the previous article regarding fills.

Weight, Dashes, and Arrows are among the additional options accessible in the line color picker that are not present in the fill menu.

Selecting the Line Options entry at the end of the color picker menu opens the Line section of the Format Shape task pane, which provides even more options for adjusting the appearance of solid and gradient lines. You can modify characteristics such as the corners, arrows, and caps (line ends) in addition to the lines themselves.

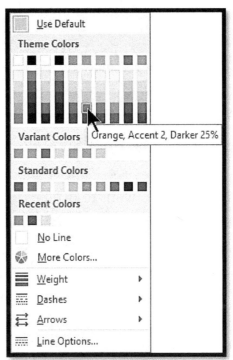

To Enable the line's Color Picker Visible

Select a choice from the list below.

- On the Home menu, select the Line button located in the Shape Styles group.
- Click and hold a shape. Point at the Styles button located on the little toolbar to select Line.

To Open the Format Shape pane's Line section

Select a choice from the list below.

- After the color picker opens, select Line Options and hit Line.

- From a shape's context menu, choose Format Shape to add a line.

To Utilize a Solid Color for a Line, carry out one of these actions:
- After launching the color picker, choose a color icon from the Theme Colors, Variant Colors, Standard Colors, or Recent Colors sections.
- In the Colors dialog box, choose the Standard tab and choose your preferred color.
- Use the tint slider in the Colors pane after launching the Colors dialog box, choosing the Custom tab, and then selecting the appropriate color.
- Select RGB or HSL from the Color model list, click the Custom tab, and then type values to choose the desired color.
- In the Format Shape task box, opt for Solid line. Then, click one of the aforementioned ways and the Fill Color button.

To Modify a Line's Appearance

First, select one of the following after launching the color picker:
- Upon pointing to Weight, select a line weight.
- When you point to Dashes, hit a line pattern.
- Once you have pointed to Arrows, tap on the type of arrow.

Utilize the Format Painter

The functionality of Visio's Format Painter is similar to that found in other Microsoft Office applications. It enables you to copy not only basic formatting but also more complex elements such as themes, variants, effects, and Quick Styles.

Copying and Formatting to a Single shape

- o Select the shape whose formatting you wish to duplicate, and then select the Format Painter button from the Home tab's Clipboard group.

Or

Click and hold a shape. Press the Format Painter button located on the little toolbar.

- o Select the shape that will receive the formatting.

Formatting to Multiple shapes simultaneously

- o Double-click the Format Painter button located in the Clipboard group on the Home tab after selecting the shape whose formatting you wish to duplicate.

Summary

In this section, we covered several key topics: aligning and spacing shapes, applying predefined themes and variants to pages or entire diagrams, using effects and Quick Styles, filling shapes with solid gradients, applying colors and patterns to specific shapes with pattern fills, and utilizing the Format Painter.

Chapter 7

Create Network and Data Center Diagrams

Creating network diagrams is one of Visio's most popular uses. With Visio, you can design photo-realistic rack diagrams that display the real-time status of your equipment or create simple, streamlined representations of network connectivity.

Visio 2016's Standard version offers two main templates for network diagrams: Basic Network Diagram and Basic Network Diagram - 3D. The Basic Network Diagram template includes modern two-dimensional (2D) shapes that are compatible with Visio 2016 themes. The Basic Network Diagram - 3D template features three-dimensional (3D) shapes that are exact replicas of those used in Visio 2010 and earlier versions.

The Standard version's 3D templates and the Detailed Network Diagram are included in the Professional edition. Rack Diagram, Active Directory, and LDAP Directory templates are included in Visio Professional.

Generate Fundamental Network Diagrams

A vital component of many networks is an Ethernet network. The Visio Ethernet shape is a brilliant shape that conceals its complexity with simplicity. This figure shows the appearance of an Ethernet form when it is dragged onto the design page on the left side.

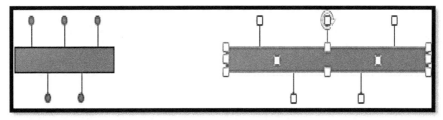

With five lines and dots at the ends, you could believe that an Ethernet segment can support a maximum of five network devices. A segment can actually accommodate up to 64 linked devices.

The key lies in the yellow control knobs that appear when you select the shape. In addition to the control handles at the ends of the five lines, two sets of control handles emerge as pairs in the shape's center. As you drag one of the central control handles, another appears, allowing up to 64 handles. Although this image only shows seven connected devices and eight possible connection ports, there will still be two control handles within the center of the Ethernet segment.

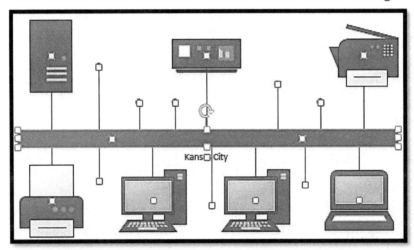

The two-dimensional computer and network shapes are compatible with the themes and effects discussed in the previous chapter, "Add style, color, and themes." For example, the image shown here uses Variation 4 of the Zephyr theme. Additionally, the computer shapes have the Art Deco bevel effect applied, while the two network segments feature the Dark Red, 8 pt, and Accent Color 6 glow effect.

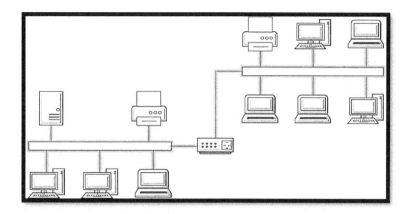

Most shapes in the Basic Network Diagram stencils represent standard internal-use computers and network components. The Detailed Network Diagram template, discussed in the article below, includes stencils that depict most components of a wide area network.

Avoid deleting any unnecessary control handles that appear outside the Ethernet segment shape, as this will delete the entire Ethernet segment. Instead, you can hide unwanted connections by sliding those control handles back inside the Ethernet shape. These handles are visible when you select the network segment.

Steps to Create Diagram of an Ethernet Network

- o Shift the Ethernet shape onto the page.
- o Scroll around the page to place various computer and network device shapes.
- o After choosing the Ethernet form, drag and paste the yellow control handle onto each machine or network shape.

How to Add More than Five Devices to an Ethernet shape

Slide the yellow control out of the middle of the Ethernet shape.
To Adjust an Ethernet Segment's Width or Length

Once the Ethernet form has been selected, drag any white adjust handles.

Develop Detailed Network Diagrams

Additional stencils for creating more intricate designs are included with the Detailed network diagram template in Visio Professional.

The primary differences between the Detailed Network Diagram and Basic Network Diagram templates are shown in this figure by the two versions of the Shapes pane. The template for a basic network diagram (left) has just two stencils. These two, as well as five additional stencils, are part of the Detailed Network Diagram template (seen on the right).

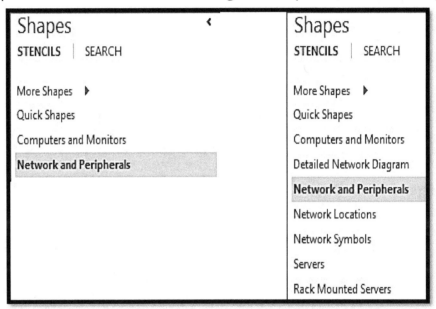

When using the Comprehensive Network Diagram template, if a toolbar appears when you drag the pointer to the upper portion of the Shapes window, slide the divider between the title bar area and the shapes section down to reveal all the stencil titles. To create a realistic representation of your network, use the 17 shapes in the Servers stencil to represent various server types. A similar set of 17 shapes can be found in the Rack Mounted Servers stencil. The remaining stencils include numerous symbols representing network hardware and locations.

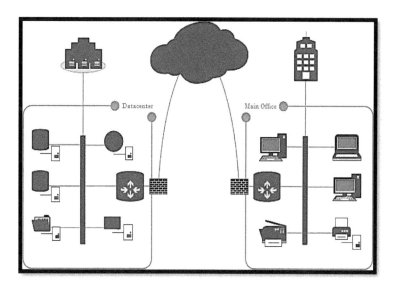

To Symbolize a Business Network

- o Drag and drop local area network and PC shapes into the page.
- o Join the shapes of devices and local area networks.
- o Link the wide area network device shapes together using fluid connectors and the Comm-link shape from the Network and Peripherals stencil.

Utilize 3-d Equipment shapes

The earlier chapters demonstrated the modern, two-dimensional computer and network shapes in Visio 2013. That being said, keep in mind that traditional three-dimensional shapes are still available in the Basic Network Shapes - 3D and Detailed Network Shapes - 3D (Professional edition only) stencils.

An insightful comparison of the two shape designs can be found in this image. The network components in the diagram's lower half are shown in 3-D form, while the network inside the diagram's upper half is depicted in 2-D forms. There is no right or wrong style—both are offered, so you may select how your diagram will look.

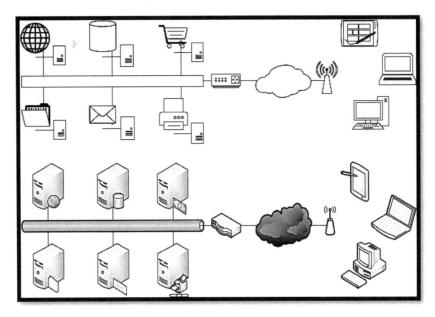

The following two elements could also affect your decision when selecting the appropriate style for your diagrams:

- o The majority of the shapes and stencils that equipment vendors supply are designed in three dimensions. (See "Where can I find other network shapes?" in this chapter's sidebar.)
- o The 2-D network forms were created with specific Visio themes in mind. These designs seem more straightforward than the 3-D shapes whenever no theme is used, yet

Sidebar: Where are Additional Network shapes Available

The network shapes included with Visio may resemble your servers, routers, and other equipment, but they are generic shapes and cannot be exact replicas.

To create more lifelike diagrams, you can get thousands of printable Visio stencils and shapes from three main sources:

- o For their products, Image Network and computer equipment vendors commonly give shapes, most of them photo-realistic shapes. To locate shapes specific to a particular seller, browse or search the website.

- o Some companies make and sell generic Visio shapes, while others are product-specific.
- o Shapes for network gear and computers have been created by people. Some charge for their artistic creations, but many give them away for free.

Create Rack Diagrams

It's common to find the equipment depicted in the schematics from the earlier articles outside of the data center or wire closet. To create diagrams of the equipment in those backstage areas, you utilize some of the forms from computer and network stencils. Visio Professional does, however, also provide additional stencils that you will need. An important backstage element of rack diagrams is their forms, which this piece explores in terms of their peculiar behavior.

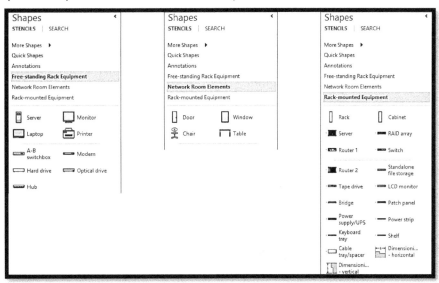

Let us first define a rack diagram. A scaled drawing is a rack diagram. When shapes on a page are proportionate to the size and scale of the page, the drawing is said to be scaled. The pages in the Rack Diagram template already have a scale factor selected, however one may add scaled drawing pages to any layout.

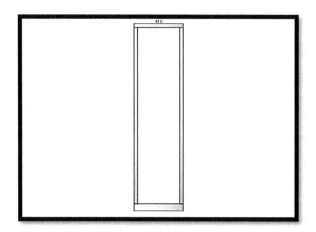

As seen in the subsequent examples, every device you drag into a rack displays its height in rack units and the shape of the rack.

Here, we show you how to rack-mount a 2U Power Supply/UPS. Based on what you learned about connection points in Chapter 2, "Build diagrams," the following three elements in the illustration suggest that the rack and the equipment shape have active connection points, despite the absence of precise one-dimensional (1-D) shapes: the bottom corners of the Power Supply/UPS form have green squares. The words "Glue to Connection Point" appear in a ScreenTip.

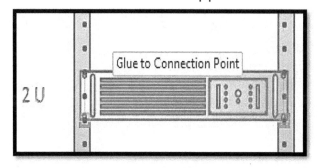

This graphic highlights a unique characteristic of rack equipment shapes and a few other Visio types: although they appear to be two-dimensional, they behave similarly to lines, dynamic connectors, and other one-dimensional shapes. This 2-D/1-D combination results in shapes that resemble the actual equipment they represent but can be attached to specific points on a rack's edges.

The exact positioning of the gray squares, which indicate connection points, on both corners of the rack at intervals of one U allows U-sized forms to be positioned in the same manner as their real-world counterparts. There are many other forms of adjustable racks, such as the Server design that is seen in the two sides of the figure below. A server's default height whenever dragged into a rack is 8 U, as can be seen on the left side of the image. But because it has two-dimensional features, you may resize handles and change the server's height, as shown on the right. Because of the shape's design, your network diagram ought to seem a lot like the actual thing.

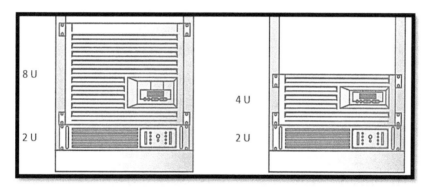

We depict the potential appearance of a full rack in this picture. Navigate to the left portion of the figure, where the U dimensions of every discernible shape are located. The dimension is different on the right.

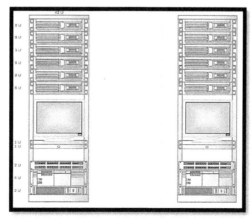

Creating a Rack Diagram

- o You can drag a Rack and a Cabinet shape into the page.
- o Before affixing the shapes to the rack, drag and drop the Free-standing Rack Equipment and Rack-mounted Equipment stencils onto the page.

To show or hide the U height for racks and equipment forms attached to racks

After doing a right-click on a shape or a rack, select one of the following options:

- o Press the display **U** sizes button.
- o Select hide to conceal **U** sizes.
- o After choosing a form, adjust the height of equipment mounted on racks using the resize handles on the shape.

To include a rack diagram page in addition to an existing network diagram

- o Add a page to the diagram.
- o Set the scale factor on the new page to 1:20 for a diagram in metric units or to 1" = 1'0" for a figure in US units.
- o Drag and drop rack and accessory shapes onto the screen.

Sidebar: Meaning of Scaled Drawing

Visio rack diagrams are scaled drawings. The page size of the rack shapes is designed to be proportional to the drawing scale of the page. At a 1:1 page-to-rack ratio, each shape would be "life-sized," occupying the same amount of space on the page as it would in a physical rack. With a 1:10 scale option, each unit of measurement in your drawing corresponds to 10 units in the real world. For example, a 1:10 scale could mean that 10 mm on the page corresponds to 1 cm in reality. For US measurements, a 1"=1'0" ratio means that every inch on the page represents one foot in the real world.

Scaled diagrams are also included in Visio floor plans, though often at a smaller scale to allow each page to depict a larger area. While a US-based floor plan might be created at a size of 12" or 14" to 1 foot, a conventional metric floor plan might be produced at a scale of 1:25. The Drawing Scale tab in the Page Setup dialog box displays the scale for a drawing. The image shows three examples of this tab: on the left are the four preset scale types, in the center is a selection of architectural scale factors in US units, and on the right is a selection of metric scale factors.

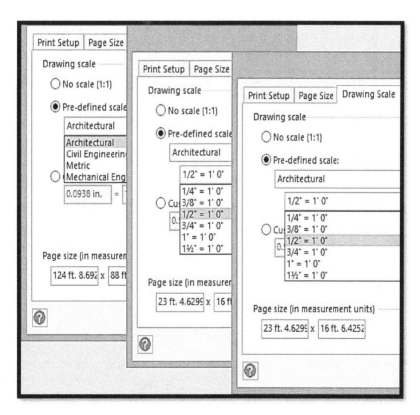

Additionally, you can select a custom scale, input numbers, and add units to create a personalized ratio for the diagram.

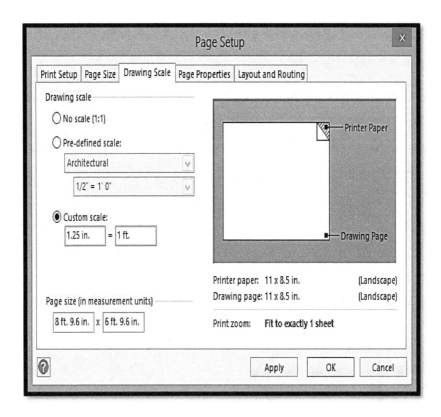

Modify the Drawing scale

Real-world illustration: You've created a rack diagram with three racks, but you need to add a few more. However, there isn't enough space on the drawing page for additional racks. Do you have to start a new diagram from scratch? No, you don't. Scaled drawings can easily accommodate such modifications. Simply change the scale factor, and Visio will adjust the diagram accordingly.

For example, if you have the drawing in this image and would like to add three more racks, you will need more space on the page. The Drawing Scale tab in the Page Setting dialog box indicates that the scale of this metric drawing is now 1:10.

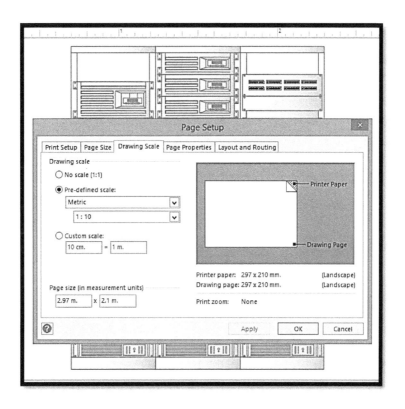

After that, you can double the scale to a ratio of 1:20 to get the desired outcome. This makes it clear that you have more room to work. The rack is tiny by this measure.

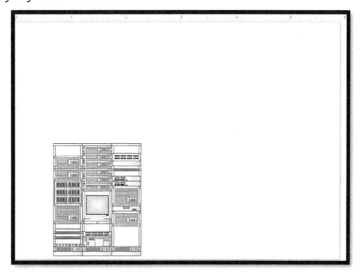

To access the Drawing Scale tab of the Page Setup dialog box

- o Select Drawing Scale from the page name tab's context menu.

To modify an architectural diagram's drawing scale

- Open the Drawing Scale tab.
- Select Architecture, then choose Pre-defined scale and click the arrow.
- Tap the arrow next to the scale factor and select a factor between 3/32" = 1' 0" and 1' = 1' 0".

To modify a Civil Engineering diagram's drawing scale

- Open the Drawing Scale tab.
- Select Civil Engineering, then choose the Pre-defined scale and click the arrow.
- Click the arrow next to the scale factor and select a factor from 1" = 1" to 1" = 100' 0".

The drawing scale of a metric diagram needs to be adjusted

- Open the Drawing Scale tab.
- Select Pre-defined scale and click the arrow, then choose Metric.
- Click the arrow next to the scale factor and select a factor from 1:1000 to 50:1.

To modify a mechanical engineering diagram's drawing scale

- Turn on the Drawing Scale tab.
- Click on Mechanical Engineering, and then pick the arrow and the pre-defined scale.
- Select a factor by clicking the scale factor arrow, which ranges from 1/32:1 to 10:1.

To create the drawing unscaled

When the Drawing Scale tab appears, select No scale (1:1).

Sidebar: Improve your Network diagram

Here are some suggestions to improve your network diagram:

- Utilize data connecting. to connect the diagrammatic equipment's asset IDs, serial numbers, and other inventory data to a worksheet or database.

- To enable the equipment to display real-time status information, connect it to a nearby real-time data source or an actual time source and use the data graphically.

- Install network and panel patching. To simply hide or display the cabling, try placing it on a different layer.

- Include information about each rack shape in the network inventory report, including the positions of the other keys.

- A hyperlink to the equipment and racks might be added.

- After that, users without Visio can view and interact with the diagrams by publishing them online or on Microsoft Sharepoint.

Run Computer and Network reports

In the following chapter, you'll discover how to utilize shape data to run reports that emphasize the key data features of shapes on the drawing page. As a preview, this subject matter showcases three preconfigured reports using Visio 2016 network diagrams. For example, this graphic illustrates information about network devices.

	A	B	C	D	E	F	G	H	I
1				Network Device					
2	Displayed Text	Network Name	IP Address	Subnet Mask	MAC Address	Network Description			
3	Branch Office 1	Branch_1				Branch Office 1 :LAN			
4	Branch Office 2	Branch_2				Branch Office 2 :LAN			
5		Branch_2	10.0.12.11			Ethernet LAN			
6		Branch_2	10.0.12.12			Ethernet LAN			
7		Branch_2	10.0.12.13			Ethernet LAN			
8		Branch_2	10.0.12.14			Ethernet LAN			
9		Branch_2	10.0.12.15			Ethernet LAN			
10		Branch_2	10.0.12.16			Ethernet LAN			
11		Corporate	10.0.5.1			WAN			
12		Branch_1	10.0.5.101			Ethernet LAN			
13		Branch_1	10.0.5.102			Ethernet LAN			
14		Branch_1	10.0.5.103			Ethernet LAN			
15		Branch_1	10.0.5.104			Ethernet LAN			
16		Branch_1	10.0.5.105			Ethernet LAN			

The analysis shown in this picture provides additional information you need about the hardware in your network.

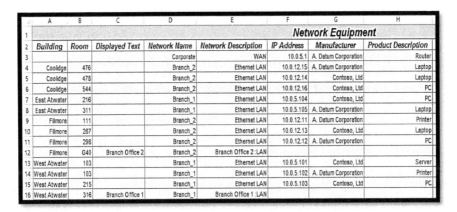

	A	B	C	D	E	F	G	H
1							Network Equipment	
2	Building	Room	Displayed Text	Network Name	Network Description	IP Address	Manufacturer	Product Description
3				Corporate	WAN	10.0.5.1	A. Datum Corporation	Router
4	Coolidge	476		Branch_2	Ethernet LAN	10.0.12.15	A. Datum Corporation	Laptop
5	Coolidge	478		Branch_2	Ethernet LAN	10.0.12.14	Contoso, Ltd	Laptop
6	Coolidge	544		Branch_2	Ethernet LAN	10.0.12.16	Contoso, Ltd	PC
7	East Atwater	216		Branch_1	Ethernet LAN	10.0.5.104	Contoso, Ltd	PC
8	East Atwater	311		Branch_1	Ethernet LAN	10.0.5.105	A. Datum Corporation	Laptop
9	Fillmore	111		Branch_2	Ethernet LAN	10.0.12.11	A. Datum Corporation	Printer
10	Fillmore	267		Branch_2	Ethernet LAN	10.0.12.13	Contoso, Ltd	Laptop
11	Fillmore	298		Branch_2	Ethernet LAN	10.0.12.12	A. Datum Corporation	PC
12	Fillmore	G40	Branch Office 2	Branch_2	Branch Office 2 :LAN			
13	West Atwater	103		Branch_1	Ethernet LAN	10.0.5.101	Contoso, Ltd	Server
14	West Atwater	103		Branch_1	Ethernet LAN	10.0.5.102	A. Datum Corporation	Printer
15	West Atwater	215		Branch_1	Ethernet LAN	10.0.5.103	Contoso, Ltd	PC
16	West Atwater	316	Branch Office 1	Branch_1	Branch Office 1 :LAN			

Whenever you needs information about PCs rather than network hardware, Visio provides the report shown in the image.

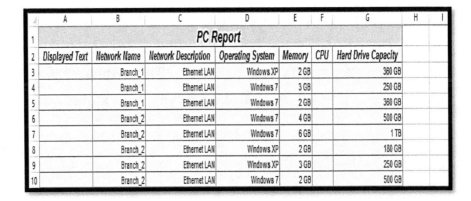

	A	B	C	D	E	F	G	H	I
1				PC Report					
2	Displayed Text	Network Name	Network Description	Operating System	Memory	CPU	Hard Drive Capacity		
3		Branch_1	Ethernet LAN	Windows XP	2 GB		360 GB		
4		Branch_1	Ethernet LAN	Windows 7	3 GB		250 GB		
5		Branch_1	Ethernet LAN	Windows 7	2 GB		360 GB		
6		Branch_2	Ethernet LAN	Windows 7	4 GB		500 GB		
7		Branch_2	Ethernet LAN	Windows 7	6 GB		1 TB		
8		Branch_2	Ethernet LAN	Windows XP	2 GB		180 GB		
9		Branch_2	Ethernet LAN	Windows XP	3 GB		250 GB		
10		Branch_2	Ethernet LAN	Windows 7	2 GB		500 GB		

Summary

This chapter guides you through the steps to create rack diagrams, design both basic and complex network diagrams, use 2-D or 3-D equipment shapes, adjust the drawing scale, and generate computer and network reports.

Chapter 8

Add Data to Your Diagrams

Working with Shape Data

While you can use various diagramming programs to create attractive and functional drawings, Visio stands out when compared to these alternatives. In addition to placing objects on a page, Visio allows users to store data within shapes. This data can then be used to modify nearly any aspect of the diagram's behavior or appearance. A data-driven Visio design becomes a powerful tool for conveying ideas and information by visualizing and responding to data values.

Understanding Shape Data

Shape data encompasses all the data fields that each Visio shape can have. Some of these fields act as repositories for displaying or reporting information. Additionally, the appearance and behavior of shapes are influenced by the values in other data fields, which can be used for various purposes.

Below is a list of the eight different shape data field types in Visio 2016, along with information on what may be entered and how data values can be added.

- **Numbers**
- **Strings:** That is to say, you are free to enter any character you choose.
- **Fixed list**: input lists from which you must choose.
- **Varying List**: a list from which users can select options and add values by entering them into the data field.

- **Duration**: one of the five time units supported by Visio, which are seconds (es), minutes (em), hours (eh), days (ed), and weeks (new), used to indicate a time value. The user types in any of these acronyms for time units after entering a value.
- **Dates**: Users have two options for entering dates: manually or from a calendar.
- **Currency:** is a phrase used to describe the amount of money that is expressed in units of currency according to the user's region and language preferences within Windows; figures are entered.
- **Boolean**: Users select a boolean value (True or False) from a list.

View Shape Data

To view shape data, the main tool is the Shape Data window. You can perform a great deal of stuff with the shape data window. It may be placed to float in any spot on the drawing page and adjusted in size to show as many or as few fields as needed.

Docking the window to a certain location can also be accomplished by dragging it to any drawing window boundary. The pushpin icon located in the window's header can be used to turn AutoHide on or off once the window has docked. Whenever you're not using the window, if AutoHide is enabled, it "rolls up" into the header.

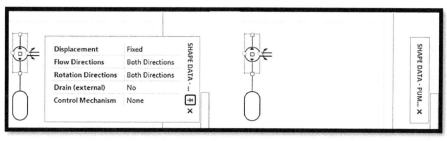

With Visio, it's crucial to keep in mind that data is necessary; the majority of stencils have pre-populated data fields.

Sidebar: An Alternative Way to View the Shape Data

Certain Visio shapes, especially older ones, offer an alternative method for visualizing shape data. These shapes have a Properties option in their shortcut menus, accessible by right-clicking. Clicking Properties opens the Shape Data window for these shapes, similar to using the Data submenu method.

Although the window and dialog box appear slightly different, both allow you to view and update data. For example, the Shape Data dialog box for the Fluid Power Pump/Motor 1 shape, shown in the following figure, was opened by selecting Properties from the shortcut menu. This can be compared to the equivalent Shape Data window illustrated here.

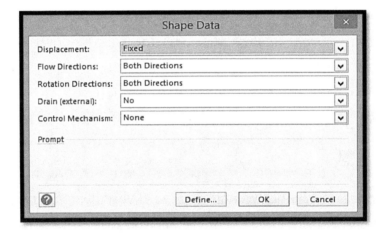

To get the Shape Data window, simply perform a right-click on the shape, navigate to Data, and choose Shape Data.

How to Open The Shape Data Window

Select a choice from the list below.

- Drag a Shape Data window's header to a point near one of the drawing window's edges to dock the Shape Data window inside the drawing window.

- You can dock the Shape Data windows as distinct windows by dragging their header past the edge of the drawing window.

Shutting the Shape Data Window

Initially, try any of the following:

- Click the Close button (X) located inside the Shape Data window's border.
- After doing a right-click in any area of the Shape Data window, select Close.
- (Under the Professional Edition only) Only in the Professional Edition Uncheck the Shape Data Window dialog box located in the Data tab's Show/Hide group.

Sidebar: Locating the Shape Data Window

The Shape Data window frequently opens in the same spot inside the main Visio window as when it was last visited.

However, you could wonder why the window didn't open in light of the following two situations:

- If a PC has several monitors, the Shape Data and Visio windows may open on separate monitors.
- Any open Shape Data windows in Visio will close when you choose Data from the shortcut menu and then Shape Data. Maybe this wasn't what you were expecting, if you didn't know the window was open and you're not sure why it didn't display.

Because the shape data on the Submenu functions like a switch, this behavior will occur. There may be a slight variation in the icon that appears following Shape Data. However, that depends on whether the Shape Data window is open or closed.

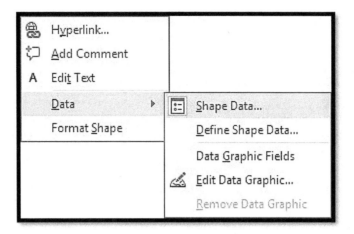

Modify Shape Data

The window allows you to switch to the modified data value in addition to allowing you to view the data that you entered into the form. As Visio rules are dynamic and heavily dependent on the type of data and formatting provided to each shape data field, you will notice that some shape data fields behave differently from others whenever you do this.

For instance, you cannot enter text in the currency or number fields in Visio. Moreover, the only data you may enter is the number plus one of the five useful time unit acronyms found in the duration box.

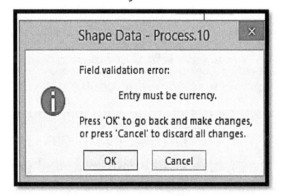

The methods by which you can enter data also depend on the kind of data that each field accepts. While most field types simply allow text or numeric input, some provide other options as well.

For example:

While utilizing date fields, the user can pick a date from a calendar. After you click the arrow at the right end of the field within the status field, a list will appear.

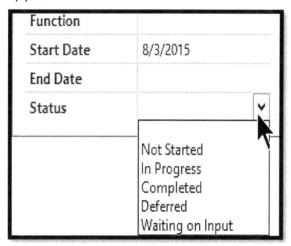

More than just one shape's worth of data can be changed at once. That being said, nothing expressly says this. The Shape Data window will display the fields shared by all of the shapes you have selected if you select several shapes. Any data values that display come from the anchor shape in your selection.

When multiple forms are selected, all of your changes are applied to all of the selected shapes. Because this feature has the potential to be extremely harmful or intense, vigilance is needed.

If you choose multiple shapes, but none of them contain standard fields, Visio shows No Common Data Fields inside the Shape Data box.

To Input Data into a Text box

Begin by attempting any of the following:

- o   Fixed list: Tap the text field to input any character you choose.
- o   Quantity: You can enter numbers by clicking here.
- o   Variable list: Simply click the arrow located at the right end of the field to select a value. Values or numbers can be entered after clicking the arrow.

Duration: Input one of the following five-time unit abbreviations: es, em, eh, ed, or ew. This must be followed by a number.

Date Take one of the following actions:

- o   After clicking in the field, enter a date that adheres to the regional date format requirements.
- o   Choose the preferred date from the calendar after clicking the arrow.

Currency: input a currency or number. Whether a currency separator is used or not,

The Boolean: Tap the arrow to show the True or False option.

The Shape Data window allows you to leave a field empty after inputting data

Select an option from the following list:

- o   Select Tab.
- o   Press Enter.
- o   Click to select a location outside the field.

Adjust the Shape Data Field Attribute

With the Shape Data dialog box, you may create a whole new shape or modify the properties of an already-existing shape data field.

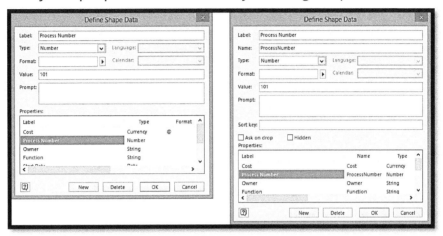

The dialog window on the left in the above image is the one that most Visio users see when they use the program. The one on the right will appear and provide a number of additional possibilities if Visio is in development mode.

The following features are present in every data field in both dialog box versions:

- o **Type**: any of the eight groups specified in the chapter's "Understand Shape Data" section before it. Chooses the format that user-entered data will be displayed in (various field types have distinct format possibilities).
- o **Value**: the data that the user enters or defines whenever defining a shape.
- o **Prompt**: In the Shape Data window, a ScreenTip shows up each time the user navigates to the shape's name.
- o When in developer mode, Visio displays the properties in the following list. While some of these properties are primarily for

programmers or developers of Visio solutions, one or two may be useful for power users.

- o **Name**: This is the internal name used by Visio developers (underscore characters are acceptable). It can be the same as the Label, but you cannot use spaces or special characters in the Name field.

- o **Sort key**: Visio knows what order to display the fields in the Shape Data window based on the alphanumeric value entered in this field.

- o **Add on drop**: If this option is selected, Visio will show the Shape Data dialog box whenever a user drags a shape with this field on a page or copies a shape with this field.

- o **Hidden**: Visio hides the field and stops it from showing up inside the Shape Data window or dialog box if this option is selected. By using a formula depending on other data values, a Visio solution developer can change the value of the hidden attribute, displaying or hiding a field under different circumstances.

Select an option from the list below to launch the Define Shape Data Dialog box

- o Choose a shape from the right-click menu, then choose Data to define shape data.

- o From the Shape Data window, choose Define Shape Data from the right-click menu.

To view the properties of a different shape data field

Scroll up or down in the lower section of the Define Shape Data dropdown menu until you find the desired field, then select the field name.

This is how to get rid of the dialog box for Define Shape Data. First, attempt one of the following:

- o Click "OK."
- o Tap Cancel to end the session.
- o Select the Close button in the upper-right corner of the dialog box.

Modify Shape Data Field Attributes

Understanding how to adjust the attributes of existing data fields and create new ones will help you fully utilize Visio's powerful and adaptable data features. This section will cover the former, while the latter will be discussed in the next section. You may adjust almost every field property using the Define Shape Data dialog box, as detailed in the previous section.

To Adjust the Characteristics of a Shape Data Field

- o Open the Define Shape Data dialog box.

- o Scroll to the preferred field in the lower section of the dialog box, and then choose the field name.

- o Enter a new value.

Define Shape Data Fields

You may add data fields to shapes you design or forms that are created using Visio stencils. In the Define Shape Data dialog box that you used in the last topic, you can accomplish both by choosing the New   icon.
If Visio is in development mode, you may choose an inner shape name and a sort key value. Select a data type and label the new field, at the very least (see "Understand shape data" earlier in the chapter). In

addition, prompt wording, type-specific format selection, and default value specification are available.

Insert fields

One common method of utilizing shape data is by displaying data values on a shape. For example, organizational charts often include information from various shape data fields. In this topic, you will learn a simple way to visualize information on any shape.

After instructing Visio to insert a field, select a specific field from the Field dialog box, as shown here. "Shape Data" is the first entry in the Category section on the left side of the dialog box. When you choose that entry, Visio presents a scrollable list of all the shape data fields.

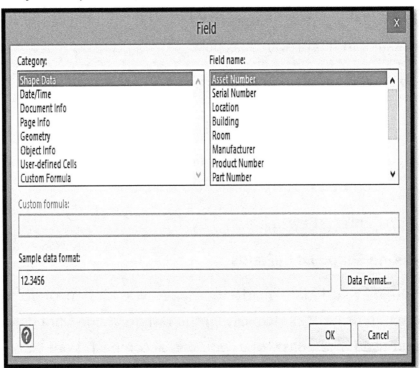

Whenever you select the location field, the Floor/Hr information appears inside the shape's text box.

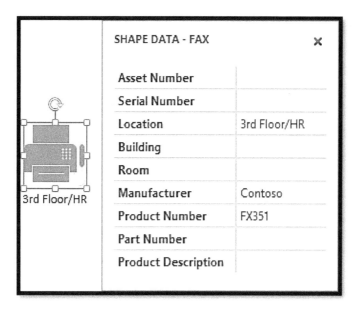

In our previous example, the Category section of the Field dialog box lists seven additional data categories besides Shape Data. Each category provides a variety of data values that can be inserted and displayed from different areas.

You can perform any of the following actions as examples:

- In the title block on the backdrop page, provide the author of the document or the most recent edit information.
- Incorporate shape width or additional geometry information to guarantee that the exact numbers are consistently displayed on the shape.
- Incorporate a special formula into a shape to represent a computed outcome.

Use these procedures to then insert the value from the shape data field into the shape.

- Select a shape.
- On the Insert tab, select the Field button located under the Text group.

- In the Category area of the Field dialog box, tap Shape Data.
- In the Field name area, choose the name of a field whose content you want to display.
- Click "OK." Text appears in the text area of your shape or shapes.

The Steps to add a document property to a shape

- Draw a shape

- In the Field dialog box, select Document Info and choose a field to insert.

- Click OK.

Run Predefined Report

Once the data has been entered, how can you use it to make your Visio diagram even more useful? The reporting tool in Visio is one of the simplest ways to accomplish this. With Visio templates, you may run the basic reports and generate custom reports. The Inventory report that most Visio diagrams offer determines how many shapes in a design originate from each master in a stencil.

Inventory		Inventory	
Master Name	Quantity	Master Name	Quantity
Database	1	Database server	1
Decision	1	E-Commerce server	1
Document	3	Ethernet	3
Dynamic connector	13	File server	2
Process	7	Laptop	4
Start/End	2	Mail server	1
		PC	5
		Printer	2
		Router	1
		Server	1
		Web server	1

Moreover, many templates contain various context-specific reports in addition to the inventory report.

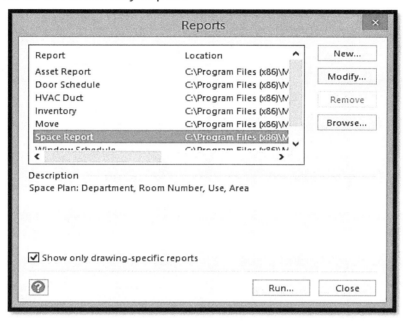

When executing the Visio reports, you have four options for output.

- By creating a Microsoft Excel workbook in this manner, Visio will open Excel and display the structured report output. The report data can be edited from this point on.
- **HTML**
- Visio Shape
- **XML**: Visio creates an XML file with the structured report. The data in the report may be edited or imported into an application that understands XML.

One advantage that is exclusive to the Visio shape export format is that it allows you to amend the report without requiring deletion and re-uploading in case you add or remove shapes or change the data values within them.

This is the procedure to run a report that is stored in a drawing.

- Go to the Reports group on the Review tab and hit the Shape Reports button.
- To open the Reports dialog box, tap the name of the required report. Next, click Run to open the Report Run dialog box.
- Hit OK to exit the Run Report dialog box after selecting the preferred output type.

To carry out a report that isn't stored in a drawing

- Select the Reports button from the Reports dialog box.
- After selecting the desired report definition files, hit Open.
- Select "Run" from the Reports dialog window.
- Hit OK after selecting the preferred output format in the Run Report dialog box.

To make updates to the report within the Visio shape

- Select "Run report" by doing a right-click on the report shape.

Create or Adjust Reports

By using the Report Definition Wizard, you may create and modify new reports. The wizard will be launched by selecting the Create or Edit button located in the Reports dialog box.

	Master Name	Displayed Text	Status	Owner	Function	Start Date	End Date	Cost
		Flowchart Report						
	Master Name	Displayed Text	Status	Owner	Function	Start Date	End Date	Cost
	Database							
Count	1							
Total								
	Decision	Candidate accepts?	Not Started	Candidate		5/5/2016		$0.00
Count	1							
Total								$0.00
	Document							
	Document							
	Document	HR Policy Manual						
Count	3							
Total								
	Process	Log hiring request	In Progress	HR Admin		4/7/2016		$0.00
	Process	Prepare job description and screening questions	In Progress	Hiring Manager		4/7/2016		$0.00
	Process	Advertise open job	In Progress	HR Admin		4/9/2016		$0.00
	Process	Interview candidates	In Progress	Recruiter		4/18/2016		$0.00
	Process	Select a candidate	Not Started	Manager		4/25/2016		$0.00
	Process	Make job offer	Not Started	Recruiter		4/30/2016		$0.00
	Process	Hire candidate	Not Started	Recruiter		5/7/2016		$0.00
Count	7							
Total								$0.00
	Start/End	Hiring need reported						
	Start/End	End						
Count	2							
Total								
Grand Total								$0.00

On the wizard's initial page, as shown in the above picture, you designate the positions of the shapes that you wish to report on.

Use the Advanced option on this page to select which shapes should be included in the report.

Creating a Report Definition

- On the Review tab, select the Reports group and then click the Shape Reports option.
- In the Reports dialog box, select New.
- Enter the required information on the pages of the Report Definition Wizard.

To change a report's definition that already exists

- To modify a report, click its name after launching the Reports dialog box and selecting the Edit button.
- Adjust the pages of the Report Definition Wizard as needed.

Summary

This chapter discussed the steps for creating, editing, and executing shape data as well as inspecting, changing, and setting shape data fields and attributes. It also covered inserting fields. We will now start visualizing your data in the upcoming chapter.

Chapter 9

Visualizing your Data

When a visitor views a Visio diagram you created, they can gain a lot of knowledge about the subject from the shapes you used, how you placed them on the page, how they are connected, and more visual clues. The five components of this topic demonstrate how well information visualization can disclose various aspects of the narrative. A straightforward rack diagram can be made into an invaluable resource for comprehending server characteristics with the use of Visio data graphics.

SHAPE DATA - SERVER	✕
Height in U's	2
Height	3.5 in.
Location	Row 1 Rack 2
Manufacturer	Contoso, Ltd.
Product Description	database server
Network Name	sql-sales-01
IP Address	10.0.1.51
Operating System	Windows Server 2016
CPU (MHz)	3
Memory (MB)	2048
Status	OK
Administrator	Anna Misiec

In this chapter, we will use this data to demonstrate the following
- Server name and IP address
- Server Status
- Operating system

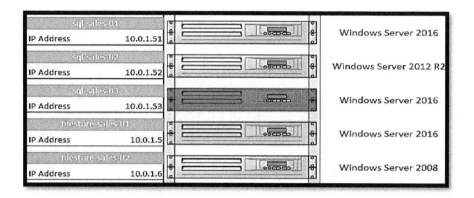

Display Network and Data Center Performance

Data graphics are used in this example to identify each process (numbers appear above the upper-right corner of each shape) and to show various measurements of process quality.

The following details are included in this graphic:

- The average number of days for each stage is shown in a progress bar across the bottom of each work form.

- A warning icon appears in the shape's lower-left corner if a step takes five to nine days, or ten days or more to complete.

- The hue of the shape denotes whether a step is being reviewed or is improving.

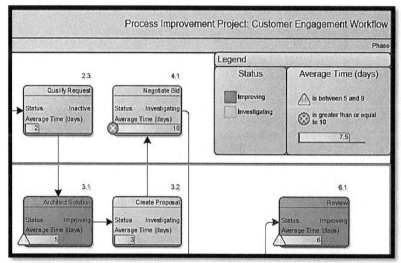

Manage Casino Operations

The kind of near-real-time data that a casino manager might see in Visio to keep an eye on important actions are depicted in this picture. Even though running a casino isn't exactly what your job description calls for, there are some important procedures that you should be aware of.

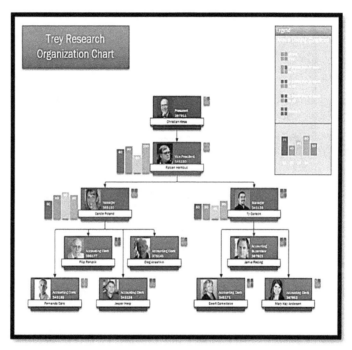

In this organization chart, we included two key performance measures.

- An emblem consisting of blue and gray squares illustrates each employee's progress toward their annual training goal.

- A bar graph displaying quarterly performance data is featured among the three red management forms. Note that the bar graph is a single graphic item that compares information from four shape data fields.

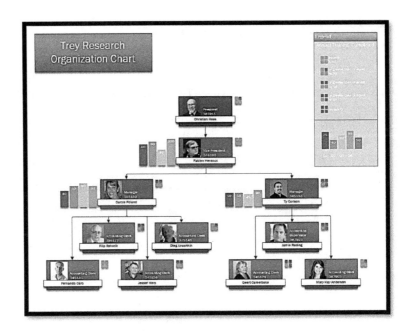

The legend is created by Visio automatically in the upper-right corner of the page, but you can change its text and other components. The font color and explanations were changed in this example.

Assess Risks

A portion of the process map made with the TaskMap Visio add-in is shown in this image.

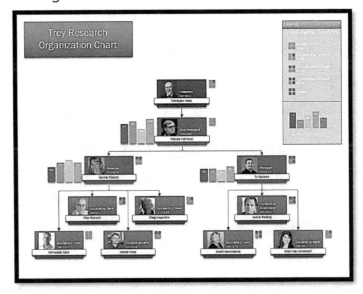

The middle three activities of a sales proposal process are represented by the TaskMap, and data graphics illustrate the two elements of risk management that follow:

- Yellow triangles and green diamonds represent hazards and controls, respectively. Each numbered triangle corresponds to an item on a master list of risks, while each numbered diamond denotes the risk-mitigation measure implemented by the company. (An organization might use a formal risk management system or a simple worksheet to manage the initial list of risks and controls.)

The organization has identified a risk but has not implemented a control measure for a task, as seen in the middle, increasing the severity of the risk.

- Tasks marked with red arrows exceed the specified time limit of 30 minutes.

Create Data Graphics

The next chapter will walk you through an easy way to add data graphics to shapes that include data from an external file or database. However, in order to link to other data, using data graphics is not necessary. Data that has been manually entered into your forms can still be visually represented. For every data visualization you create, you can add one or more visual elements.

Every graphic object has an associated data field that displays data in one of the following formats:

- **Callout**: A stylized text box that is used to show text and is often accompanied by such an icon

- **Icon**: Set up to five icons that visually represent different values or ranges of values.

- **A data bar**: is one of many different ways that numerical data can be represented visually, including pie charts, graphs, progress bars, star ratings, and other visualizations.
- **Color by value**: There is a way to alter the color of a form according to the data field's contents in the shape.

The options available on the Data tab allow you to create and utilize data graphics. The Data Graphics gallery and a few buttons on the Data tab will be muted (unavailable) if you haven't connected your graphic to any external data. These regions aren't shown in the images of the Data tab that are displayed here.

Add Data Graphics

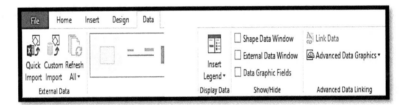

However, you must use the Advanced Data Graphics button on the tab's right end in order to create data graphics in an unlinked diagram.

To access the Data Graphics gallery, click the Advanced Data Graphics icon. There is a Make New Data Graphic button there. Choosing a data field is the first step in producing a visual item. Which shapes were selected whenever you clicked the Generate New Data Graphic button determines which data fields are available. You will see a list similar to ours in the upper half of this figure if the shape you select includes numerous similar data fields.

However, if a collection of distinct shapes is selected, you will see a condensed list similar to this one in the lower half.

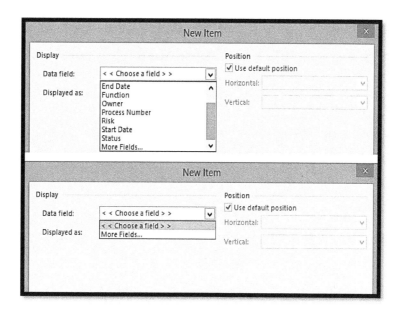

To create more intricate data visualizations in any situation, utilize the More Fields entry, which is displayed in this image's two halves. Rather than basing a graphic on a shape data field, for example, you might base it on a computed result or on a feature of the document or page.

Selecting one of the four visual item types is your next step after selecting a data field.

As is once more the case with Text, Data Bar, and Icon Set lists, the initial three graphic categories present a range of choices.

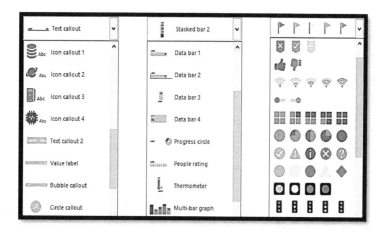

The data visual options that you will need in the next topic are shown in this graphic. Indicate the value, or range of values, that corresponds to each icon when choosing an icon set.

Even though each indicator in this image has a specific value, you have a lot of flexibility in deciding what the conditions are for each flag. It is possible to:

- The list in the center column can be used to establish a range of values for each icon and condition.
- More complex values can be entered utilizing the list on the right rather than merely typing a figure or text into the box.

The fourth type of data visualization, called Color By Value, associates a color with the data values from the selected field.

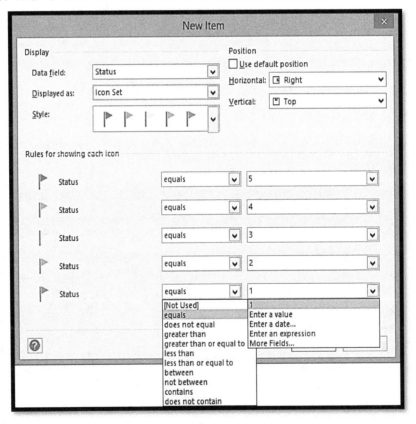

There is flexibility in configuring the icon set graphics.

Selecting a Field for Data Visualization

- To open the Create Data Graphic dialog box, select one of the following actions:
  - On the Data tab, choose Create New Data Graphic from the Advanced Data Graphics menu under the Advanced Data Connecting group.
  - If a shape has no data graphic and you right-click it, you can edit it by selecting Edit Data Graphic from the context menu.
- Pick the "New Item" button.
- In the New Item dialog box, choose the Data field arrow. Then, hit the field name to begin seeing it.

Creating a Text Data Graphic

- After selecting the desired field, click Displayed as, and then choose Text.

- Press the name of the desired text callout and then the Style arrow to choose it.
- Adjust the parameters in the Details section configuration (not necessary).
- Select a precise location for your data graphic using the Horizontal and Vertical choices, or select the Use default position option (not necessary).
- Choose OK to close the dialog boxes for the New Item and New Data Graphic, and then hit OK to exit the New Item dialog box.

Here's how to Create a Data Visualization

- Hit the Data Bar after selecting Displayed as and selecting the field you want to see visually.
- Tap on the name of the chosen data bar, and then click the Style arrow.
- Changing the Minimum Value, Maximum Value, and other setting settings in the Details section is optional.
- Check the box labeled "Use default position" or select an item from the Horizontal and Vertical categories to select a specific position.
- To dismiss the dialog boxes for the New Item and New Data Graphic, choose OK. Then, hit OK to close the first dialog box.

To Create An Icon set Data Graphic, Follow these steps

- Click on the field that you wish to see, then the Displayed as arrow and Icon Set options.
- Select the Style arrow to select the desired icon set.
- Select the appropriate criterion from the list in the Rules to display the center column of each icon section, and then input values in the section's right column.

- (Details optional) (Details optional) Check the Use default position box or select an item from the Horizontal and Vertical categories to select a specific position.
- Hit OK to dismiss the New Item dialog box and select OK to close the New Data Graphic and New Item dialog boxes.

Adding Color to the Value Data Visual

- Select Color by Value after choosing the field you wish to see and clicking Displayed as.
- Hit the Coloring Method arrow to select each color that represents a single value or a range of values. This step is optional.
- Modify or leave the values in the Value, Fill Color, and Text Color fields under Color assignments.
- To dismiss the New Data Graphic dialog box, click OK after selecting OK to clear the New Item dialog box.

Create Graphic Data Legends

Before accessing the Data Graphics gallery, you must select one or more shapes because you can only load or remove data graphics from preset   shapes.

After picking your forms, you can navigate through the options in the gallery's Available Data Graphics section by using the arrows. This section is shown here to give you a live sample so you may explore a range of graphics before deciding on one.

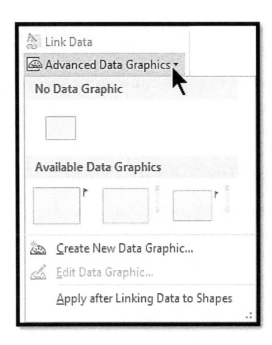

Adding a Data Graphic to a certain Shape or Shapes

- To build a gallery of data graphic options and thumbnails, navigate to the Data tab, enter the Advanced Data connection Group, and then pick Advanced Data Graphics.
- From the Advanced Data Graphics gallery, select the data graphic you want to utilize by clicking on its thumbnail.

To Remove a Data Graphic from a Specific Shape or Shapes

- Start by accessing the advanced data graphics gallery. Next, pick the None thumbnail from the category of No Data Graphic.

Modify Data Graphics

The location and style of data visualizations are determined by a set of modifiable settings. Though not every component of a data graphic may be controlled without using code, the Visio 2016 user interface provides tools to implement numerous alterations through the Edit Data Graphic dialog box.

Any graphic element that is a part of the given data graphic is listed in the upper half of the Edit Data Graphic context menu. You can change, add, or remove any visual component. The bottom portion of a dialog box contains the feature set for the data visual as a whole.

Steps to Modify Data Graphic

- Right-click on the visual data thumbnail in the Advanced Data Graphics gallery and choose Edit.

Or

Choose Data, then from the context menu of any shape that contains the data graphic you want to change, choose Modify Data Graphic.

- To update a graphic item, select it in the Edit Data Graphic dialog box by selecting it and then clicking the Edit Item button.

Or

To modify a click, double click on it

- After making changes to the item using the Edit Item dialog box, click **OK**.
- Change the values in the Default location, Display choices, and Apply changes to sections of the Edit Data Graphic dialog box (optional).
- Before exiting the Change Data Graphic dialog box, click the Apply button (optional) to see the changes inside the diagram.
- Select **OK**.

Adjusting a Data Graphic's Name

- Choose the thumbnail of the data graphic from the context menu to open the Advanced Data Graphics gallery. Then, hit Rename.

- Enter an alternative name, then select OK.

Copying a Data Graphic

- Choose Duplicate from the menu when you right-click the thumbnail of a data graphic in the Advanced Data Graphics gallery.

To Choose Every Shape that Utilizes a Particular Data Visual

- Right-click on a data graphic thumbnail in the Advanced Data Graphics gallery, and choose Shapes that utilize this Graphic from the context menu.

Eliminating a Data Graphic

- Choose Delete from the menu when you right-click the thumbnail of a data graphic in the Advanced Data Graphics gallery.

Designing Data Graphic Legends

How to add a legend to a data visualization
- Click the Insert Legend button on the Data tab, located under the Display Data group.
- Select between horizontal and vertical.

To Adjust the Data Legend Visualization

- Tap inside a legend entry to add new text.
- To move a legend entry, click on it and drag it to a new location.

Changing a Data Visual's Legend

- To begin repositioning the legend, hit the Legend title located in the visual data legend header.

Elimination of Data Legend Visual

Initially, try any of the following:

- After selecting the word Legend from the data visual legend's heading, hit the Erase key.
- To choose Cut, use the shortcut menu that appears whenever you right-click the word Legend.
- Select the word Legend from the context menu with a right-click, and then select Cut from the Clipboard group on the Home tab.

Summary

This chapter takes you through the steps involved in producing and implementing data visuals, establishing and modifying graphic data legends, and enhancing the efficacy of diagrams.

Chapter 10

Connection to External Data

By connecting your Visio diagrams to data and visualizing key data features, you can transform them into interactive dashboards. Whether you need to display the status of servers and printers in a network, show weekly attendance for each employee in an organizational chart, or provide a real-time office layout indicating who is in or out today, you can achieve all this and more by combining data linking and graphics.

A new tool in Visio 2016 is called Quick Import; it makes connecting to Excel data and applying data visualizations easier. If you have needs beyond what Fast Import can provide, you can use the Custom Import process to link to nearly any data source.

Understand Data Connecting

To link a diagram to data and then display that data, there are four steps involved:

- Attach the diagram to a data source.
- Attach particular shapes to information entries.
- Create a suitable data visualization.
- Utilize the data in a graphical format.

All four processes are automatically completed by Quick Import, which will be explained in the following section. If you don't use Quick Import, you must complete each step manually. However, Visio provides wizards to assist with the first two steps. Regardless of the method you use to link to external data, the connection is dynamic. Refreshing the diagram updates the shape data fields and any applied data visuals. Consequently, your Visio design can serve as the primary access point for your data. Both data connection methods display data in the External Data window, as shown in this example.

By using Custom Import, Visio explicitly opens the External Data panel; however, Quick Import does not always do this. You can manually open or close the window by selecting or deselecting the External Data Window check box found in the Show/Hide group on the Data tab.

Name	Reports To	Title	Employee Num	Extension	Annual Tra	Q1	Q2	Q3	Q4
Christian Hess		President	367911	101	80				
Fabien Hernoux	Christian Hess	Vice Presid...	345180	125	100	80	90	60	100
Carole Poland	Fabien Hernoux	Manager	385150	115	50	40	80	70	80
Ty Carlson	Fabien Hernoux	Manager	345138	111	40	50	68	59	72
Fernando Caro	Carole Poland	Accountin...	345165	120	100				
Filip Rehorik	Carole Poland	Accountin...	395177	124	40				
Jesper Herp	Carole Poland	Accountin...	345156	117	60				

Page-1   VBackground-1   All ▲   ⊕   Drag rows onto the page to link data to existing shapes or to add new linked shapes.

Sheet1$A1:M12

Utilize quick import

Quick Import is the fastest way to link your shapes to external data if your data is already in Excel. For an example of the simplicity of the Quick Import wizard, see the figure, which includes a portion of a Blue Yonder Airlines organizational chart. The open Shape Data window displays the usual fields for a Visio organization chart. Although the Name field indicates that the selected shape represents Carole Poland, the other four shape data columns show default values.

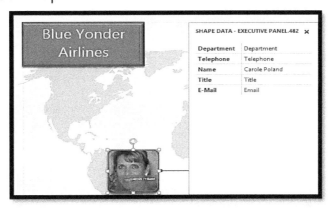

This is the diagram to which we wish to connect it.

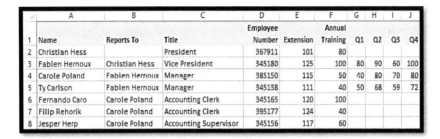

	A	B	C	D	E	F	G	H	I	J
				Employee		Annual				
1	Name	Reports To	Title	Number	Extension	Training	Q1	Q2	Q3	Q4
2	Christian Hess		President	367911	101	80				
3	Fabien Hernoux	Christian Hess	Vice President	345180	125	100	80	90	60	100
4	Carole Poland	Fabien Hernoux	Manager	385150	115	50	40	80	70	80
5	Ty Carlson	Fabien Hernoux	Manager	345138	111	40	50	68	59	72
6	Fernando Caro	Carole Poland	Accounting Clerk	345165	120	100				
7	Filip Rehorik	Carole Poland	Accounting Clerk	395177	124	40				
8	Jesper Herp	Carole Poland	Accounting Supervisor	345156	117	60				

It operates immediately as soon as the Quick Import Wizard launches and is pointing at the Excel data file.

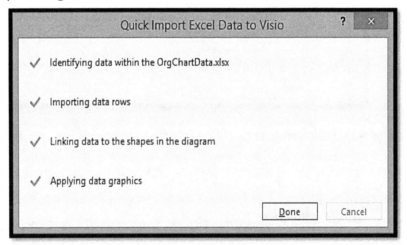

This is how it will ultimately appear.

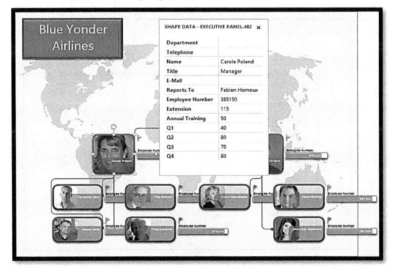

It is important to understand that Quick Import bases its data visualization options and applications on an analysis of the data fields' shapes. It might or might not select relevant data graphics and appropriate fields. See "Use visual data choices for linked data" further in this chapter for information on adjusting the applied graphics.

To learn how the associated data graphics and diagram might be updated whenever the Excel data changes, check "Refresh linked data" later in this chapter.

Steps to Using the Quick Import

- Select a choice from the list below.
  - Select the Data tab, External Data category, and hit Fast Import.
  - In case the External Data window is open and no data sources are associated, select Quick Connect Data to Shapes icon.
- In the Data Selection dialog box, pick an Excel workbook by selecting the Browse button, and then click Done.
- Select Quick Import Excel Data to Visio by clicking Done in the dialog box.
- Press Ctrl+Z to undo the work.

Utilize Custom Import

Although all four data connection and visualization steps described in "Understand data linking" earlier in this chapter are finished with Fast Import, there will be times when you want to link straight to a data source. When your data is kept elsewhere other than Excel that is one obvious example. Even if the data is in Excel, you might prefer to link manually if you want more control over the linking and viewing.

Custom Import allows you to link to data from any of the following repositories:

- o Microsoft Excel spreadsheet
- o database utilizing Microsoft Access
- o List of the Microsoft SharePoint Foundation
- o database utilizing Microsoft SQL Server
- o A repository accessible by ODBC or OLE DB

Connect the data to your diagram

Once the Data Selector wizard knows where your data resides, you can use that Link to narrow down your options.

This image displays the Excel data selection screen at first. Decide the worksheet or range you want to use as the limit for the source by selecting it from the list. Excel opens and allows you to choose the required range whenever you hit the Choose Custom Range option. You can select which columns and rows to exclude from the wizard screen that follows the one in this picture.

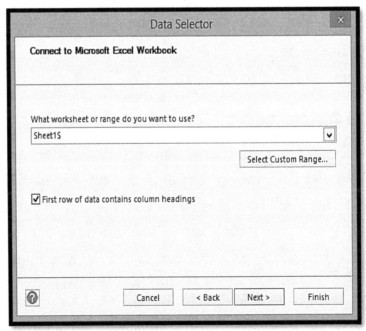

This is the initial selection page for the information contained in a SharePoint list.

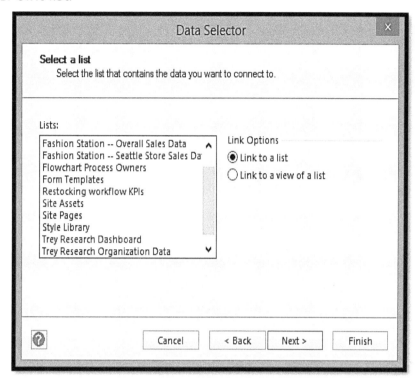

Similar filtering and selection features are available from other types of data sources.

For some types of data sources, you can select which field—or set of fields—uniquely identifies each data record. Establishing a unique identifier in your data is beneficial if you want your diagram to reflect any subsequent changes to the data in the repository.

Here, we show you how Visio looks through your data and selects what appears to be a unique identity. You can overrule the program's decision-making, even if it usually makes a good one, by ticking or unchecking the boxes in the figure.

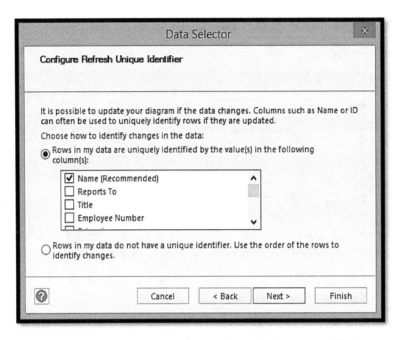

You may choose the option at the wizard's bottom if the data does not have a unique value in each row. After the connecting procedure is complete, the relevant data is shown in the External Data window 1.

Take one of the Subsequent actions:
- o Select Custom Import from the Data tab's External Data category.
- o From the External Data window's context menu, select Data Source with the right mouse button, and then press Add.
- Select the data source type that you want to connect to by tapping on it and then selecting Next on the Data Selector wizard's first page.
- Complete all remaining pages in the Data Selector wizard (the exact pages depend on the type of data source). After the procedure is complete, if the External Data window isn't open already, it will open and display the newly linked data on the data tab.

Connect Data to your Shapes

Data rows in the External Data window can be linked with shapes on the drawing page using any combination of the three linking options. **One may:**

- Drag and drop data onto an existing shape.
- Automatically connecting shapes with data
- Use the data to create a shape.

Regardless of the method you use, the end result is usually a one-to-one relationship between data rows and forms. One-to-many links, however, can also be made.

On the basis of this, you may link:

- **One shape to multiple data sources**: Certain fields may be linked to values in a list stored in SharePoint, and other fields with the same format could be linked to data stored in a SQL database.
- **Multiple forms from one data row**: It is possible to link many shapes on the same page—or other pages—to the fields of the same data row.

Dragging Data to Pre-existing Shapes

Dragging a row of data onto an already-existing shape results in the following:

- It provides mismatched shape field names
- data is added to fields in the shape that share the same name.

To link data to a present shape

- Drag a data row to a shape by clicking on it in the External Data box.

For Data to be Automatically Connected to Shapes

- Under the Advanced Data Linking section on the Data tab, select Connect Data.
- Hit **Next** after selecting Selected shape or All shapes on this page on the first page of the Automatic Link wizard.
- In the Data Column section, pick a column name from the list, then click **Next**. In the Shape Field section, select a field name.
- Select "Finish."

This is how to Use Data to Make Shapes

Drag a data row into a drawing page blank to create a new shape and add data.

When using this method, before dragging the data row, select where the master Visio should draw the new shape.

- If the master hasn't been selected previously in the form Data box, click it to start building a new form from there.
- From the External Data pane, click and drag a data row to a desired location on the drawing page.

Regulate Connected Data

- You should be aware of a few administration and maintenance elements before selecting between Custom Import and Fast Import.

Determine Connection

- Once shapes are linked to external data, there are situations when it becomes vital to identify which rows and shapes are connected.

To Identify the Shapes that are linked to a Data Row

- Right-click the row in the External Data window and select Connected shapes from the context menu.

To find out which rows a shape is attached to

- Right-click the shape after selecting Data and Display Connected Row.

Adjust Column Settings

For imports that are more complex than the simplest, you may find that you need to change the way data is associated with shapes:
You could require fewer columns in your graphic than what your data source contains. You may want to display the shape data fields in your diagram in a different order than the columns in the data source. The type of data that was imported might not be correct; consider a date field that was imported as text, for example. For each of these issues, Visio offers solutions.

Adjust the Column Parameters before Connecting

- You may access Column Settings by doing a right-click on the External Data window.
- Use the Column Options dialog box to modify a column's data type, rename it, add or remove fields from view, or rearrange the columns' order. Hit OK after making your changes.

Eliminate the Data Linkages from Diagrams and Shapes

It could be essential to unlink data forms or even a schematic from a data source. All you have to do is click backspace after selecting it.

Separating a shape from its data

- Go to the shape's context menu and select Data to unlink from a row.

Disconnect off a Diagram's Link to a Data Source

Select one option from the list below.

- To remove the data from the External Data window, click the tab containing the desired data and then select Remove from the context menu.
- To delete something from anywhere in the External Data window, utilize the right-click menu and select Data Source.

Remove Data Links from Diagrams and Shapes

There is an option to show or hide the Data Graphic Fields task window.

Initially, try any of the following:

- Select the Data Graphic Fields check box located on the Data tab's Show/Hide group.
- Select Data Graphic Fields after selecting Data from the context menu of any shape.
- Upon performing a right-click anywhere within the External Data window, you can select Graphic Data Fields via the context menu.

To Navigate to an Alternate Data Visualization

- Select a field name from the Data Graphic Fields task pane. Next, select the Data Graphics gallery's thumbnail of the data graphic you want to utilize.

To Reposition a Presently shown Data Graphic

- Tab on the name of a field within the Data Graphic Fields task pane.
- Select Position from the Data tab's Data Graphics group.
- Select from the following options:
    - Click on a preset menu item to select it.

- Select the desired location by using the Horizontal or Vertical click buttons.

To Adjust a Present Data Graphic

- Tap on the name of a field within the Data Graphic Fields task pane.
- On the Data tab, select one of the following actions from the Data Graphics category:
  - Choose **Configuration**
  - Tap More Data Graphics after showing the Data Graphics gallery.
- Click OK after making the required adjustments in the Edit Item dialog box.

Utilize Graphic Data Options to Connect Data

Update Connected Data

Once you link a diagram to data and integrate data graphics, your diagram becomes a window into your data. The diagram's graphics refresh in tandem with any changes to the data because both the data visuals   and   their   link   are   dynamic. Data for diagrams can be programmed, updated manually, or updated on a regular basis.

The first two possibilities are described here, but the programming option is outside the scope of this book:

Manual Refresh: If your diagram has multiple data sources linked to it, you may choose to update each source individually or all of them by selecting the Refresh All option.

Automatic Reload: Use the choices in this dialog box (Configure Refresh) to set up automatic refresh. The data from the provided source is then updated by Visio anytime your diagram is open, at the time interval you specify.

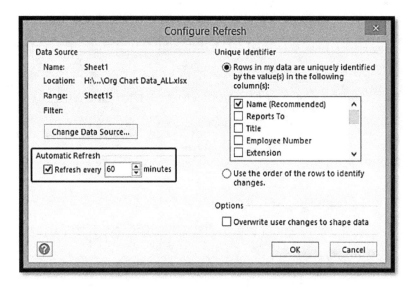

Updating Data Manually for Every Connected source

- On the Data tab, hit the Refresh All option located underneath the External Data category.
- In the dialog box for refreshing data, hit close.

Updating Data for a Single Linked source by Hand
- On the Data tab, hit the Refresh All arrow under the External Data category, and then choose Refresh Data.
- To reload a source, tap it in the Refresh Data dialog box, then select Refresh and Close.

Or

In the External Data box, choose the source tab that you want to update.

- Right-click anywhere in the External Data box to select Refresh Data.

- In the dialog box for refreshing data, hit close.

To automatically refresh data for a Single Linked Source

- In the External Data window, select the tab of the source that you want to reload.
- Right-click anywhere in the External Data window to bring up the context menu. Select Configure Refresh.
- After selecting the Refresh every check box and typing a number in the minutes box, the Configure Refresh dialog box will appear. Hit **OK**.

Summary

The procedures for maintaining linked data, renewing linked data, utilizing Fast Import and Custom Import, and employing visual data options for linked data are all covered in this chapter.

Chapter 11

Applying and Utilize HYPERLINKS

Creating links between shapes in a Visio design and external resources is one of the best ways to make a diagram more helpful. As you develop or refine a drawing, try to anticipate the supplies your readers will require. Then, to enhance the viewer's experience, include those ideas into the linkages in your diagram.

A direct hyperlink may lead to a different page within the same Visio layout or website. A more complicated hyperlink can take the user to a specific set of cells on a certain worksheet in Microsoft Excel. A similar link may take readers to a particular area of a Word document created in Microsoft Word that contains information about a given graphic section.

The destination documents of your hyperlinks could be stored on a shared network drive, in Microsoft SharePoint, Microsoft OneDrive, or on another cloud storage service. Put otherwise, you can link to any electronic object, no matter where it is located.

Understanding Hyperlink

Prior to learning how to create hyperlinks, you must know where to find and how to use them in a Visio diagram. You can point at a shape that has a hyperlink and do two things, both of which are shown in this illustration. There is a hyperlink symbol displayed in the lower-right corner of the pointer.

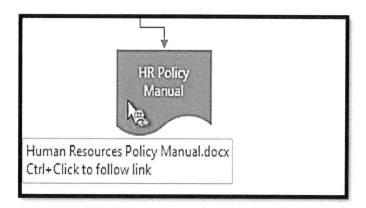

A ScreenTip including instructions on how to click the hyperlink and a description of it emerges.

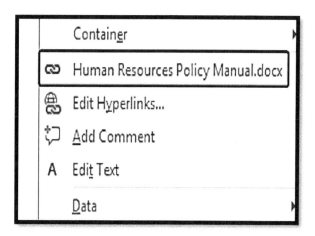

The above will appear whenever you right-click on the shape that has the hyperlink.

Select a choice from the list below.

- Press and hold the Ctrl key as you click a shape that contains a hyperlink.
- To get the description of a hyperlink, right-click on a shape that has one, then select it from the shortcut menu.

Add Hyperlinks to Improve Diagrams

Any Visio diagram may be made better with links.

For instance:

The task-related documentation such as policy manuals, other papers, online forms, or IT systems can be linked to the process boxes in a flowchart. You can create hyperlinks from an organization chart to the complete contact details on each person's corporate intranet. Every piece of equipment can be connected to warranty information, purchase histories, and service manuals via a data center map. An office floor plan can be linked to each cubicle with a worksheet for the employee's computer setup or equipment inventory.

Access the Hyperlinks Dialog box

The dialog box is where you must begin in order to add a hyperlink.

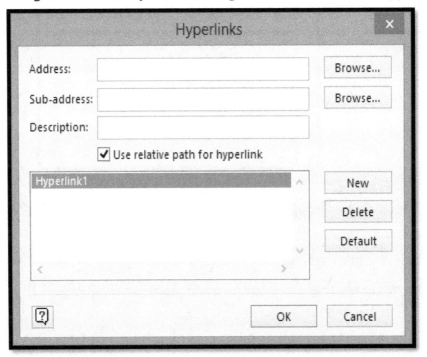

The hyperlink target is specified using the fields located in the upper section of the dialog box. The lower part of the dialog box lists any hyperlinks that are present on the shape.

To bring up the hyperlink dialog box

Begin by attempting any of the following:

- Select the Hyperlink button from the Insert tab's Links group.
- Whenever you right-click a shape, select Hyperlink from the context menu.
- Press Ctrl+K to type.

Connecting to another Visio Page

A hyperlink that leads from one drawing page's form to another has multiple applications.

You may add links to the following pages:

- Making it easier to navigate through a diagram page by page.
- To provide page navigation for numerous connected diagrams
- Include a drill-down function that allows the user to navigate from a higher-level view to a lower-level view by just clicking on a shape. (You can continue doing this for as many levels as required.)

With page-to-page hyperlinks, you can send the reader to a certain page or, on the destination page, you may connect to a specific shape.
To connect a page to an active Visio diagram, follow these steps

- Select Links in the dialog box.
- Click the target page name after selecting the subaddress field.
  - Alternatively, use the Browse button that is adjacent to the Sub-address field.
  - Select the target page's name from the Hyperlink dialog box's Page list, and then press OK.
- You can optionally type text 4 in the Description field
- and click "**OK**."

The Next Step is to link a page within another Visio diagram

- Select Local File from the Hyperlinks dialog box by clicking the Browse button adjacent to the Address field.
- When the Visio diagram you wish to link is selected, hit Open.
- Use the instructions in the step before to link to a page in a Visio diagram.

Sidebar: What's the name of a shape? Where can I locate it?

Internally, each shape in a Visio design is referred to as a sheet, and Visio ensures each shape has a distinct identifier. Each shape has a unique internal name in the format of Sheet or Sheet.n, where n is a numerical representation of the shape's internal ID. Shapes may also have names related to the original master from which they were derived, such as Process or Process.12. One way to find a shape's name is by using Visio in development mode.

To identify a shape's name, follow these steps:

- Activate developer mode, then select the desired shape.
- Click the Shape Name button in the Shape Design group on the Developer tab to open the Shape Name dialog box.

Once you have copied or noted the text that displays to the right of the Name box, close the Shape Name dialog box.

Linking the Shape on a Particular page

- o Select a different Visio diagram or leave the Address field in the Hyperlinks dialog box empty to link to the current Visio diagram.
- o Select the Browse button, which is located to the right of the Sub-address box.
- o In the Hyperlink dialog box, select the target page's name from the Page list.
- o Type your preferred shape's name in the Shape field.
- o Hit **OK** (at your discretion) after selecting the appropriate zoom level from the Zoom list.
- o (Optional) Type your content into the Description field.
- o Click **OK**.

Connect to a website

- o First, launch the Hyperlinks dialog box.
- o Enter or copy the appropriate webpage's URL.

Or

Take the Following actions:

Choose Browse after entering the Internet address in the address area. You open your browser in Visio after clicking the Browse button next to the Address box. Navigate to the intended website and then come back to Visio. In the Address section, type the address of the website, and in the Description form, write its title.

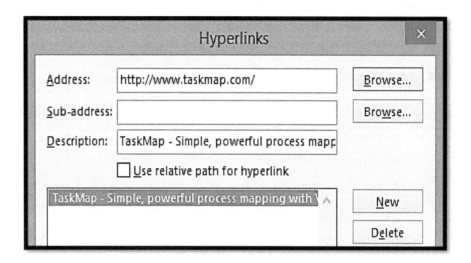

In the description area, type your words, then click "**Ok**."

Connect to a Document

Assume that one image is worth a thousand words. In that instance, including links to Word, Excel, Portable Document Format (PDF), and other documents that are essential to comprehending the context of the diagram in yours might make it much more appealing. Put another approach, you could use hyperlinks to make every Visio design you produce into the visual center where people go to get the information they require to finish their duties.

To Reference a Document

- Open the Hyperlink Dialog Box.
- Press the Browse button next to the Address column and select Local File.
- Select the file type arrow in the lower right corner of the Link to File dialog box to examine a list of file kinds.

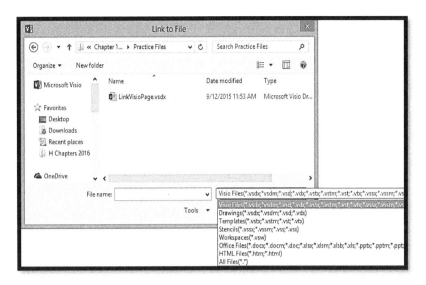

- Select Office Files or an alternative file format.
- Once the file you want to connect to has been selected, hit Open. The Hyperlinks dialog box now includes the path to the target document, and the file name serves as the default description.

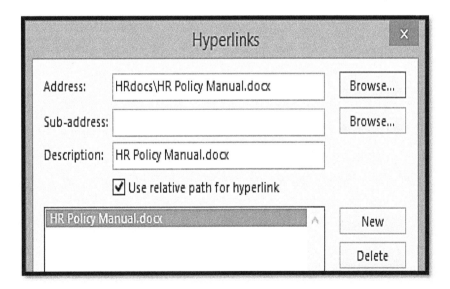

- (Optional) You may put more information in the Description area, which normally comprises the name of the selected file.
- Click **OK**.

Connect to a Particular Place inside a Document

You may be surprised to hear that there is one more potent option available if you think linking to a document is useful: creating a hyperlink to a particular location inside a document. Consider a process map where the same budget spreadsheet is referenced 13 times.

Think about the five worksheets in the budget workbook, each containing a unique collection of data. Using a generic hyperlink to open the workbook, each of the 13 hyperlinks will leave the reader to infer the location of the information required for each step of the procedure. If only the reader could click on any one of the thirteen hyperlinks to view a specific cell or collection of cells rather than having to open the workbook!

Completing these types of circumstances requires you to know how to create links to specific locations in Word documents, PowerPoint presentations and Excel spreadsheets.

You can construct your hyperlink once you have given names to particular cells or cell ranges in Excel. A hyperlink pointing to a particular cell or range will cause the corresponding worksheet to open and highlight the cell or cells in question in each case.

In Word, you can create named bookmarks in two different ways:

- It is possible to name the position of the insertion point.
- Any text, ranging from a single character to multiple paragraphs, can have a name assigned to it.

If you create a bookmark using the first technique, your Visio hyperlink will navigate to the bookmark's location on the page. Using the second technique, your hyperlink will navigate to the selected text and highlight it. While you can't name specific locations in PowerPoint, you can reference slides by their numbers or titles.

Create a Link to a Specific Location using an Office Document

- Launch the Hyperlinks dialog box.
- Click the Browse button next to the Address field and select Local File.
- In the lower-right corner of the Link to the File dialog box, click the file type button to display a list of file types.
- Select Office Files, choose the file you want to link to, and click Open.
- Enter the following details about the selected Office document in the Sub-address box:
  - The name of an Excel column or cell range
  - The name of a bookmark
  - A PowerPoint presentation number or unique title
- (Optional) Although the Name of the selected file is usually the only text in the Description box, you may add additional content there as well.
- Click OK.

Modify and Remove the Current Hyperlinks

- Links that already exist can be changed or eliminated.
- Open the Hyperlinks dialog box if there is already a hyperlink on a shape.

Begin by attempting any of the following:
- Select the Hyperlink button from the Insert tab's Links group.
- Use the right-click menu on the shape to choose Edit Hyperlinks.
- Press Ctrl+K to type.

To Modify a Connection

- Start by opening the Hyperlink Dialog Box.
- Select the link you want to change, if it hasn't already been selected. When you choose a hyperlink, its details show up in the appropriate fields at the top of the Hyperlinks dialog box.
- Change the Address, Sub-address, or Description information using the techniques described in any other section of this article, and then click OK.

How to Eliminate a Connection

- Open the Hyperlink Dialog Box.
- Select the link you want to delete if you haven't already.
- Choose Delete after selecting **OK**.

Add Numerous Hyperlinks

You can give the people who are viewing your diagrams an array of options by adding many hyperlinks to a Visio shape. A shape's hyperlink collection can contain any mix of documents, webpages, Visio pages, and other link kinds.

Visio offers three indicators when there are a lot of links:

When a shape is pointed to in a ScreenTip, the words "Many Hyperlinks" show. The right-click shortcut menu contains every link that might possibly exist. The Hyperlinks dialog box's lower section displays the descriptions of each active link.

To Add other Connections

- Open the Hyperlinks dialog box and hit the New button.
- Use any method described in this chapter to add a hyperlink, and then hit OK.

Understand both Absolute and Relative Hyperlinks

Undoubtedly, you have seen a Use Relative Path for Hyperlink check box in the Hyperlinks dialog box. If you look closely, you might have also noticed that if you haven't saved your design yet, this check box isn't available; if it has, however, it is available and selected. What is this situation about?

- **Relative Link**

A route to the destination is provided by this type of link, which presumes a given starting place. The folder on the same hard disk that contains the Visio design is called the lobby, and hyperlink targets are positioned in relation to that starting point.

Whenever the link between the starting point and the hyperlink targets remains consistent, close connections work effectively for Visio designs. However, if you need to transfer the Visio drawing file to another computer, or even just a different location on the same computer, problems could arise. In this case, you need to keep tight ties between the target files and folders and the Visio file's new location. To accomplish this, one way is to copy the entire directory structure, which includes the Visio design and its linked targets.

- **Absolute Link**

Whichever where you start, this link provides all the details you need to locate a related site.

What is the purpose of the Visio Hyperlinks dialog box checkbox in relation to any of these? Visio assumes that for a saved drawing, the path to the target of a hyperlink starts in the same folder as the Visio diagram. Visio will create a relative hyperlink based on normal procedure when you choose the location of your Visio drawing as the starting point for the route.

Although there are no complicated guidelines on whether to use relative or absolute links, it's still a good idea to take your environment and the composition of your document collection into account when creating a lot of connections in Visio. If every document you want to link to is in its proper location—on a network server or in a SharePoint repository, for example—absolute links are probably the best choice. Close connections, however, should only be used sparingly if your environment is particularly unstable or if you know ahead of time that you will be moving your Visio design and its hyperlink targets to a different computer, a CD, or a DVD.

Set the hyperlink base

You can use the hyperlink base document-level property in Visio to shift all relative hyperlinks within a document to a new location. The value you enter in the hyperlink base field will be appended to all relative links in Visio.

To adjust the connection database

- Once the Info page is open in the Backstage view, hit the Properties icon located on the right side of the screen. It's easy to miss the button with the pointer right above it.

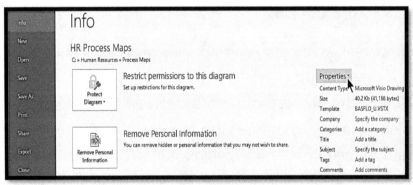

- Select Advanced Properties from the menu that appears.
- Select OK from the Properties dialog box.

To Delete the Hyperlink base

- Open the Properties dialog box.
- Select OK after removing the text from the Hyperlink base area.

Summary

This chapter explains how to define the foundation, use existing hyperlinks, add, update, and remove them.

Chapter 12

Print, Reuse, and Share Diagrams

There is a good chance that you will want to distribute a Visio diagram you have made. If a printed copy is required, Visio offers a variety of printing choices. However, you will often wish to send your diagram electronically, either in its entirety or in parts, and often to others who are not familiar with Visio. Your diagram can be exported as a PDF file, created in many image formats, or made into a Visio template.

Better more, your diagram may be saved as a fully functional audience-specific website. Visio designs may contain sensitive information, so it's important to know about the alternatives available to remove confidential material when sharing a file. The Information Rights Management (IRM) tools in Microsoft Office can be used to further safeguard your document.

Preview and Print Drawings

You can immediately check how your diagram will print by using the Visio 2016 print preview window, which displays page pictures. Printing this network diagram will require four sheets of paper due to its size and the printer's and drawing page size settings at the moment.

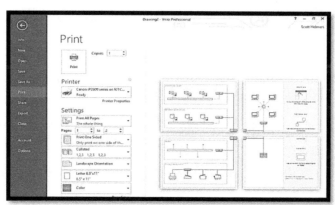

It always shows the page you are now on in your diagram in the Print page preview window. The page selection located in the lower center of the Print page can be used to preview individual diagram pages if your diagram consists of many pages. The sample picture's size can be easily adjusted by dragging the slider located in the lower-right corner. You can get assistance from Visio 2016 in rearranging items to improve the diagram's printing efficiency by using the new Move Off Page Breaks tool. If there's any remaining shape residue, you could want to shift the router slightly to the right. Here's what happened to the middle section of the print preview.

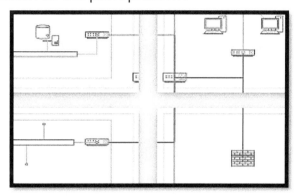

The network diagram in the first two images above was created using an 8.5 by 11-inch sketch and printer paper, using US units. Visio expanded the drawing page to accommodate network shapes larger than 11 inches wide by 8.5 inches high, therefore four printer pages are required to accommodate the enormous design. As can be observed above, when the printer paper specifications are adjusted to a size that encompasses all four drawing pages, the print preview is updated. As with other Office products, you use the first option in the Settings section to choose which portions of the current page, or a range of pages, to print.

However, Visio has two additional print options at the bottom of the button's menu:

- **No Background**: This changes whether or not the page backdrop appears in the print preview and final product.
- **Print preview and printed output:** • It is possible to omit high-quality changes. Certain effects, like reflections, for instance, can be added or removed from the Print preview and printed output.

You may find a link to the Edit Header & Footer at the end of the Settings section. Regardless of the page itself, Visio's headers and footers print data at the top and bottom of every printer page. Nevertheless, the majority of Visio documents are configured to print each drawing page on a separate piece of paper. If you would want text and images to appear on each printed page, it is recommended that you arrange them on a backdrop page.

To Display a Print Preview

Begin by attempting any of the following:
- In the left pane of the Backstage view, select Print.
- Press Ctrl + P.
- Press Alt + F, P.
- To ensure compatibility with Visio 2007 and older, use Alt+F, V.

Print out a Diagram

To print from the Backstage view, hit the Print button.
Here's how to update or add a header and footer

On the Print page of the Backstage view, select Edit Header & Footer. Adjust as needed, and then press OK.
To Eliminate Page Breaks from Shapes

On the Home tab, select the Arrange group and then click the Move off Page Breaks option.

Delete Personal Information

There is a set of metadata about the actual document in every Visio document. Visio provides some data fields (such the name of the document creator), but other data fields are left blank unless you enter values or are prefilled based on the template you use to create a document.

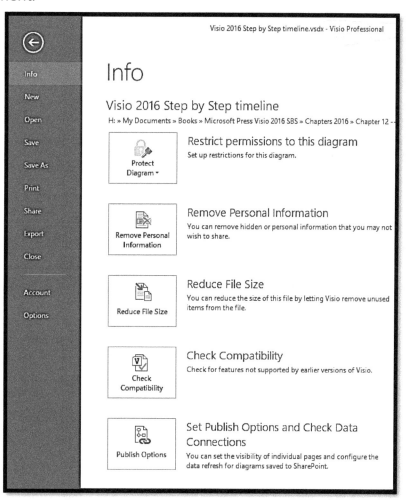

Utilize the Remove Hidden Information dialog box if your diagram will be posted publicly or if you'd like to be sure that reviewer marks, personal information, and other potentially private items are removed.

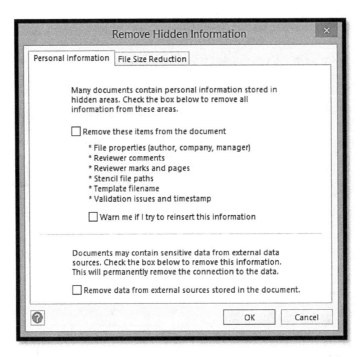

Viewing the Info page in Backstage view allows you to examine and edit the metadata fields located in the Properties section on the right side.

The Erase Hidden Information dialog box has the following three checkboxes:

- You can delete data and markup for editing and validation by checking the box in the Properties section of the document.
- When you enter certain information, a popup will appear. In the event that you inadvertently add private information to the document after erasing it, it serves to protect you.
- The data sources that this graphic has been connected to offer the option to delete sensitive information. Data from external sources saved in the document is removed by checking this box.

There are important differences, but not all of the elements that you may remove are accessible within the document attributes.

Reviewing or Changing the Properties of a Document

- Navigate to the Info page 2 in the Backstage view.
- (Optional) (Optional) To update the field's value, click on it, then enter the required information.

Or

- Select the Info button in the Backstage view, and finally hit the Advanced Properties button.
- (Optional) Enter the required data in the relevant fields.
- Hit the **OK** button.

Removal of Personal Data

- Select Delete Personal Information from the Info page in Backstage view.
- Select the options you want to remove from the Remove Hidden Information dialog box, then tap OK.

Sidebar: Meaning of Information Rights management

Visio 2016 has a new security and control function called Information Rights Management (IRM). You can help to protect the data in your Visio diagrams by limiting who can view and edit the information.

On the Info page of the Backstage view, select the Protect Document button to activate IRM in a Visio design. You may adjust the parameters in the Permission dialog box to designate which users can view or edit your diagram if you choose Restricted Access. Both those inside and outside of your organization may be named.

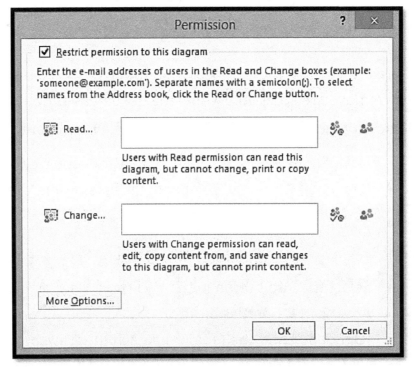

The Visio application will provide the appropriate warning or error when a user accesses a restricted document, based on who the user is and what privileges they have for the document.

If you wish to restrict access to those who are employed by your firm, select one of the Confidential options from the Limit Access menu. Both of the confidential entries include that phrase since the business name under which the author's Office 365 account is located is Visio Step by Step.

If you are a member of an organizational network, your organization's name will show up in the Limited Access section.

Create Graphics

One of the most useful features of Visio is its ability to create picture files from any or all of the elements on a drawing page. Information on the most often used picture formats may be found in the Graphic File Types section of the Export page in Backstage view.

The Save As menu will display the entire collection of graphic files.

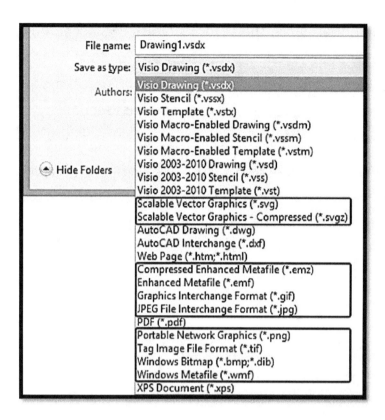

A dialog box that allows you to adjust the image format is included with the majority of image formats.

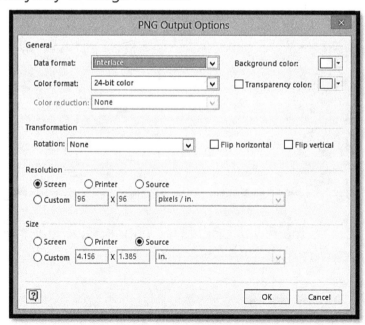

Instead of being page-oriented, Visio's image creation process is frequently shape-oriented. In other words, Visio always creates graphics from forms. Therefore, it doesn't have a built-in method for producing an image of an entire page.

To Save a Picture Using Particular shapes

- Select Change File Type from the Export page of the Backstage view.
- Under Graphic File Types, select one of the following two options:
  - Choose Save As after selecting the preferred image type.
  - Double-click the kind of image you want.
- In the Save As dialog box, select your preferred location, and then hit Save.
- Once the output settings have been adjusted based on the type of image, hit **OK**.

You can also carry out the following

- On the Backstage view's Save As tab, pick the location you want to store the file.
- In the Save As dialog box, select your chosen file type by clicking the Save as type arrow.
- After entering the intended file name, tap Save.
- Once the output settings have been adjusted based on the type of image, hit OK.

Making an Image Using Each shape on the Page

Select a choice from the list below.

- Select each shape on the page.
- To deselect every shape, tap the page's background.

263

Saving Drawing in other File Formats

Whenever you create numerous graphics files with Visio for the shapes on a single page, you may save the entire design in different formats.

Save As format name	File extension	Description
Visio Drawing	.vsdx	Visio 2016 and Visio 2013 drawing (cannot contain macros)
Visio Stencil	.vssx	Visio 2016 and Visio 2013 stencil (cannot contain macros)
Visio Template	.vstx	Visio 2016 and Visio 2013 template (cannot contain macros)
Visio Macro-Enabled Drawing	.vsdm	Visio 2016 and Visio 2013 macro-enabled drawing
Visio Macro-Enabled Stencil	.vssm	Visio 2016 and Visio 2013 macro-enabled stencil
Visio Macro-Enabled Template	.vstm	Visio 2016 and Visio 2013 macro-enabled template
Visio 2003-2010 Drawing	.vsd	Visio drawing in file format used in Visio 2003 through Visio 2010
Visio 2003-2010 Stencil	.vss	Visio stencil in file format used in Visio 2003 through Visio 2010
Visio 2003-2010 Template	.vst	Visio template in file format used in Visio 2003 through Visio 2010

Save As format name	File extension	Description
AutoCAD Drawing	.dwg	AutoCAD drawing format; file can be opened directly by AutoCAD and other CAD systems that use this file format
AutoCAD Interchange	.dxf	AutoCAD drawing exchange format; intended to provide greater interoperability among systems that do not use .dwg extensions
PDF	.pdf	Adobe Portable Document Format; accurate rendering of a Visio drawing, including most hyperlinks, that is intended to be read-only; requires free PDF viewer
XPS Document	.xps	XML Paper Specification; an alternative to PDF for creating high-quality, read-only renderings of a document; requires free XPS viewer
Web Page	.htm/.html	HTML rendering of a Visio drawing that is viewable with a web browser

To Create a PDF out of a Diagram

- Select Generate PDF/XPS from the Export page of the Backstage view.
- Press Publish after selecting the preferred location.

Or

- On the Backstage view's Save As tab, select the location you want to store the file.
- Select the Save As type arrow to choose PDF (*.pdf) in the Save As dialog box.
- After entering the intended file name, hit Save.

Adjusting PDF Output

- When the Save As dialog box appears, tap the Settings button.
- Make the necessary changes to the choices, press OK, and then choose Publish.

To Save a Diagram in a Another kind of File

- Tap the Change File Type button on the Export page for the Backstage view.
- Select from the following options:
  - Select the required file type in the Drawing File Types or Other File Types sections, then click Save As.
  - In the Graphic File Types section, double-click the appropriate picture type.
- After selecting the location, click Save.
- After confirming or modifying the output parameters based on the type of image, click OK.

Or

- On the Backstage view's Save As tab, select the location you want to keep the file.
- In the Save As dialog box, select your preferred file type by clicking the Save as type arrow.
- Choose Save after typing the names of the desired files.

Create Templates

In terms of technology, saving a diagram in a Visio template is the same as saving it in any other format specified in the previous article. Templates are covered separately in this topic despite their ease of creation because of their possible importance.

Why would a diagram be useful to use as a template? Therefore, Microsoft cannot possibly anticipate every type of diagram you might need to create, even with Visio's abundance of templates.

Furthermore, a template has the advantage of never being inadvertently altered, even though you can open a diagram and use it again in its current format. This function is essential if you distribute your template to others;

Adding a background page to one of the normal Visio templates, with your company's logo on each page, allows you to rapidly create a custom template. Alternatively, you might create a really intricate template with your own unique stencils and forms, plenty of background and foreground pages, pre-made shapes on some pages, and a disclaimer at the bottom of every page. Anything that will make a new diagram easier to understand can be added to a template; there are no limitations.

Saving a Diagram as a Template

Select the file type as Template (*.vstx) or Visio Template (*.vstx) and proceed as directed in the "To save a Visio diagram in another file format" method that follows the previous subject.

Sidebar: Where to Save Custom Templates

You can store customized templates anywhere you choose, such as on your computer if you only use them for yourself or on a server if you want to share them with other people. Although you can utilize a template by double-clicking its file name in File Explorer, Visio can be configured to provide more easily accessible custom templates by displaying them on the New page in the Backstage view.

Three distinct templates from the Trey Research Templates folder are used in the sample that follows. To instruct Visio on where to find your template folder, perform these steps:

- On the Settings page of the Backstage view, select Advanced.
- After navigating to the bottom of the Advanced options, select the File Places button.
- In the File Locations dialog box's Templates section, type the path to the folder holding the Trey Research Templates folder.

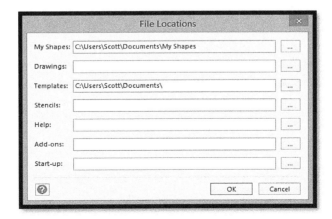

- After inputting the template path, hit **OK** twice. After restarting Visio, this should be what the Template Categories section of the New page looks like.

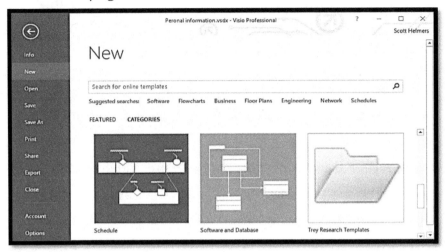

- Double-click the Trey Research Templates folder to view every template in it.

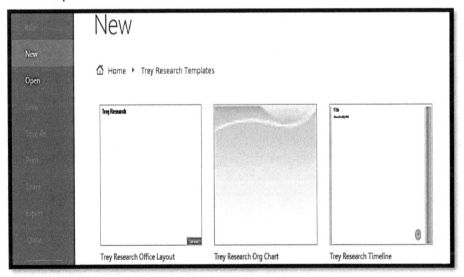

Share Diagrams by Utilizing the Visio viewer

When installing Microsoft Office 2016, the Visio Viewer is the default choice. So, even if your PC runs Office rather than Visio, you can still see any Visio diagram. Visio diagrams are seen in the browser by using the Visio Viewer, an Internet Explorer add-on.

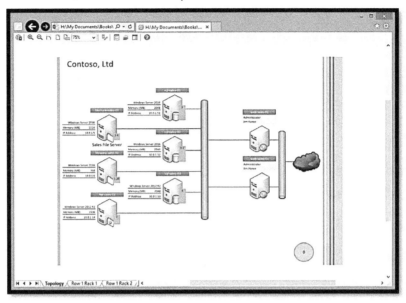

In Internet Explorer, the top-left corner has buttons to examine comments, manage layers, zoom in and out, and display shape data. If the diagram is multipage, tabs for the page names and page navigation buttons are located in the lower-left corner.

Publish Diagrams to the Web

Visio 2016 maintains a long-standing feature that lets you make a website from any diagram. You can share diagrams with others whose computers do not have Visio installed by using this capability. On a Visio website, all primary pages, a table of contents, and internal and external hyperlinks are retained.

The website is accessible through almost any web browser, but Internet Explorer has the following additional features that will make it perform better:

- You can pan and zoom through any website using the zoom and pan pan pane feature.
- Shape data is displayed in an information window.

269

- Comprehensive text search across the entire drawing.

Whether you want to share drawings with coworkers via your intranet site or publish drawings on the public Internet, the Save As Web Page feature helps make your diagrams more accessible.

Display web-published diagrams and set publishing options

Assume you have uploaded diagrams to the internet using the default settings.

These operations can be accomplished by using the navigation pane located on the left side of your browser window.

- Click Page to select a page from the list of pages contained within the diagram.

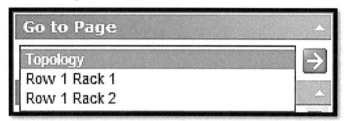

- Pan & Zoom For the viewing window, set the pan level and zoom.

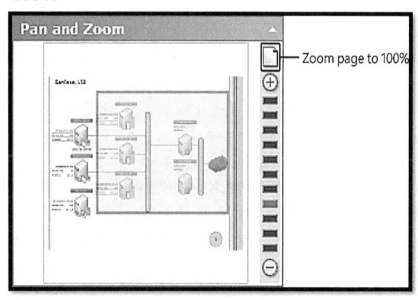

- The specifics to see the shape data.
- The pages that display the full-text search.

Creating a Webpage Using a Diagram

- Select Change File Type from the Export page of the Backstage view.
- Choose Save As after clicking Web Page (*.htm) in the Other File Types box.
- In the Save As dialog box, select the desired location, and then hit Save.

Or

- On the Backstage view's Save As tab, tap the location you want to store the file.
- Press Save after selecting Web Page (*.htm; *.html) from the Save As type drop-down selection in the Save As dialog box.

To Navigate to a Different page

- In the Get to Page pane, hit the down arrow and choose the name of the preferred page.
- Select one of the two alternatives that are given below.
  - Press the green "Go to" button to select the desired page.

To Adjust the Zoom Level

Select one of the first three Pan and Zoom pane options available:
- Press the webpage thumbnail, and then use a bounding box to draw the outline of the area of interest.
- If the rectangle on the webpage thumbnail has a red border, you can drag any of its corners.

- Decide if you want to zoom in (**+**) or out (**-**).
- Select a button to enlarge the image by x%.
- Select the page's 100% zoom option.

To Navigate through the Website

- If there isn't one on the webpage thumbnail in the Pan and Zoom box, drag to create a red-bordered rectangle.
- Use the mouse to drag the red-bordered rectangle.

Displaying Shape Data

While holding down the Ctrl key, click on the shape whose data you want to see.

To Look up Text

- Type your desired text into the Search Pages text field.
- Select any search result to see the shape that includes the term you entered.

To Click on a Link

Move your cursor over the shape containing the URL you wish to click on.

To Modify the name of a Visio-generated website

- After launching the Save As dialog box, tap the Change Title button.
- Hit **OK** and choose Save after entering a title in the Input Text dialog box.

To Change the Appearance of a Visio-created Website

- Toggle between the Save As dialog box and the Publish button.

- Make the necessary changes in the Save as Web Page dialog box, and finally press OK.

To change a Visio-Created website's Design Appearance

- Toggle between the Save As dialog box and the Publish button.
- Select the preferred format by clicking on its name in the Save as Web Page dialog box's Output formats section.
- Choose the alternate format name if you'd like inside the Provide Alternate format box. If you're using an outdated browser, this information is for them.
- Change the Display setting.
- Then choose ok

What is a website created with Visio, and where is it kept?

Visio uses the Save To Web Page function to create the homepage of the website. For every page in the drawing, it generates a supporting files folder containing webpages and images in addition to the JavaScript, XML, and other files that comprise the website.

By default, Visio puts the home page in the same Windows folder as the drawing and names it after the design. The file extension is.html. The drawing name and the supporting files folder name in Visio's English editions are the same, except the _files prefix comes first. Consider the following scenario: you use Visio and an English translation to create a webpage for a Timeline diagram (vsdx).

The following data is also included in the folder of the Visio diagram:
- The Timeline diagram .htm file
- The Timeline diagram files folder

If you want to move or duplicate your new website, you will need to move the.htm file and the accompanying files folder. Copy your webpage to any other web server, a shared file, or your company's network to make your Visio diagram accessible.

Summary

This chapter takes you through the process of constructing templates, sharing diagrams using the Visio Viewer, previewing and printing drawings, modifying graphics, saving diagrams in various file formats, and publishing diagrams online.

Conclusion

This chapter takes you through the process of creating templates, sharing diagrams using the Visio Viewer, previewing and printing drawings, modifying graphics, saving diagrams in various file formats, and publishing diagrams online.